Swimming Technique Illustrated

Written and published by Lewis Parnell Ltd
Published by Lewis Parnell Ltd
Copyright ©2013 Lewis Parnell Ltd

All rights reserved. All content including diagrams are owned by Lewis Parnell Ltd and unauthorised copying, sharing or use for financial or educational purposes, without explicit authorisation under licence from Lewis Parnell Ltd will constitute an infringement of copyright.

email: lewisparnell@btinternet.com

ISBN: 978-0-9576982-7-7

Guide to using this guide

<u>Intro</u>

This technique guide will help you identify the common faults and issues in each of your strokes. More importantly, it suggests ways to correct those faults through changes in technique, in-pool drills and out of the water activities. Quite often, a fault is caused by something unrelated happening elsewhere in the stroke and is not simply because of a lack of concentration or wrong positioning.

I've written this so swimmers can find their way through it for themselves, for parents to help their children with technique and for coaches to show swimmers their stroke, explain what's going wrong and then work with them to put things right.

Technique is the foundation of good swimming, particularly early on in your swimming career. I can't emphasise enough how important it is to get the basics right and lay down the building blocks for future success. Good technique will help you to take seconds off your swim times, help you win races and beat your competitors. A good stroke also puts you head and shoulders in front of those with untidy and irregular strokes and of course, it's cool to have a good stroke.

The guide is split into two sections. Section 1 consists of the stroke assessment cards and Section 2 contains the detailed analysis of the component parts of the stroke, fault identification and fault resolution. It would be useful if you gave the complete guide the once over before you start as this will give you the bigger picture of what I'm trying to achieve.

I've written this guide from the swimmer's perspective and from my own experience. I still hold county records from when I was competitive, some 20 years ago. I've been taught by some of the best international swim coaches and have been lucky enough to have received the best insight and knowledge on technique. Some of the best advice I have ever been given though was early on, from my coaches in the Saturday morning stroke technique sessions – they really set me on the right track. I have passed as much of this on to you as I can, especially the handy hints, the drills which will help you and the exercises and activities that you can do out of the pool. I'm blessed now that my children have an interest in swimming and have joined the local club. I've written this guide with them in mind, in the hope that they too will develop great technique which will set them up to be the best they can.

Section 1

Start with section 1 and complete an initial assessment by checking the position of your arms, legs, body and head as well as the key timing points against the accepted positions in the diagrams on the stroke cards. This will alert you to any areas you will need to concentrate on as you get to section 2. The cards provide a visual display of the stoke technique you have. Section 1 is great for:

Swimmers – you can self diagnose your stroke. See what the correct stroke should look like and replicate this in the water. Your parents, your buddy and your coaches can help you. Your coach is best placed as they have the expertise, but don't discount what your parents are telling you – they have your best interest at heart and although they do go on a bit sometimes, they do want you to succeed. They also spend hours and hours watching your stroke technique in the pool.

Parents – you are the ones who have just as much dedication as your swimmer. You spend all those hours watching your swimmer and I know you want to help. You can see so much from the balcony or side of the pool. Use this guide to help your swimmer with their technique – you will be better informed as to what should happen, what actually is happening, how you can help and how it all fits together. What I will ask you though is to be constructive, pick you moments for discussion well and discuss things with the coach if you are concerned.

Coaches – you are the ones with the expertise in all this. I never cease to be amazed at your dedication and how you bring swimmers to where they are. This guide can help you develop each swimmer's technique so they can realise their true potential. Unlimited use of the stroke cards can be provided under licence so all swimmers in your club can benefit.

Section 2

Section 2 provides the detail on the faults, what the likely causes are and how to correct them. It enables you to isolate a fault and understand what is causing it – sometimes this is not so easy to spot.

Don't forget that all swimmers are different both in terms of temperament (and this should reflect how you use this guide) and body composition. I've tried to ensure that this guide can be applied to all swimmers, whatever shape and size but I do contrast where the stroke will be different between sprinters and longer distance swimmers. Whatever your standard or whatever you are aspiring to – there's loads of information in here for you, technique is for all:

Elite swimmers - you are really talking improvements of 1% here and there, it all adds up. Technique can give you the extra which may mean the final, a medal, the title or the record. You're never too good that you can't tweak that something which gives you the advantage. There are whole academies based around giving the top-end athletes the smallest of advantage in technique. Be the best you can.

Club swimmers - technique is very important, get it right and you will reap the rewards of success - qualifying times for Counties, Regionals and Nationals, finals and medals. Watch yourself swim past others with your great technique. Be the best you can.

Tri-athletes, bi-athletes and other aquatic competitors - good technique is going to improve your overall performance. Swimming can often be the sport that you have come to the latest so technique is crucial in your success. You are probably fit as a fiddle through all that running, cycling and other activities and now building up your pool fitness, so watch out for the tips on flexibility and timing which will improve your swim. Be the best you can.

Fitness swimmers - increase your fitness and enjoyment by swimming well. Even though you might not be in it for the medals and competition, be the best you can.

This guide is about technique. I've left the training schedules, overall performance, tapers and racing strategies to your coaches. Happy swimming – with a good stroke!

Section 1

The Stoke Cards

Front Crawl

Body position and timing
It's all good apart from:
    legs too low []
    snaking at hips []
    timing is out []
    other observations …...

Head position
It's all good apart from:
    excess head movement []
    head too high []
    head too low []
    not looking 5 - 10 m in front []
    other observations ....

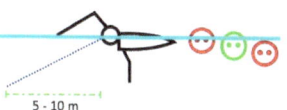

5 - 10 m

Arm entry
It's all good apart from:
    entry too short L/R []
    entry too long L/R []
    entry too wide L/R []
    entry too narrow L/R []
    not entering with thumb & finger L/R []
    other observations ....

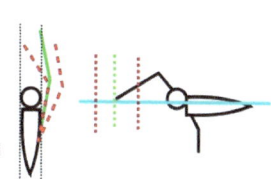

Breathing
It's all good apart from:
    not breathing into the bow wave []
    looking at the ceiling []
    looking in front []
    looking behind []
    breathing not smooth []
    excess head movement []
    other observations ....

Legs
It's all good apart from:
    legs cycling []
    kicking from knee []
    feet not flat []
    uneven kick []
    feet crossing over []
    weak kick []
    other observations ....

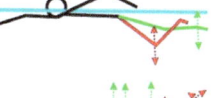

Catch
It's all good apart from:
    dropping the elbow L/R []
    straight arm L/R []
    excess pause before catch L/R []
    feathering the water L/R []
    other observations ....

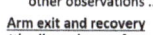

Arm pull
It's all good apart from:
    'S-curve' too big L/R []
    arm pull too wide L/R []
    arm crossing centre line L/R []
    arm too straight/ deep L/R []
    feathering the water L/R []
    other observations ....

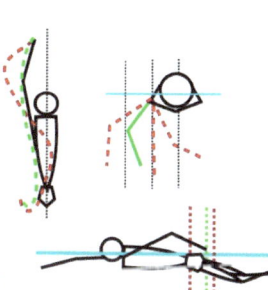

Observations:

Arm exit and recovery
It's all good apart from:
    exit too short L/R []
    exit too long L/R []
    pause on exit L/R []
    recovery arm too straight L/R []
    recovery arm too bent L/R []
    Recovery arm too high L/R []
    recovery arm too low L/R []
    other observations ....

Not under Licence - do not copy
Copyright of Lewis Parnell Ltd. All rights reserved

Backstroke

Body position and timing
It's all good apart from:
- legs too low []
- bottom too low []
- snaking at hips []
- timing is out []
- shoulders/body under rolling []
- shoulders/body over rolling []
- other observations ......

Head and breathing
It's all good apart from:
- head is too high []
- head is too low []
- excessive head movement []
- breathing is not smooth []
- other observations ......

Arm entry
It's all good apart from:
- entry too short L/R []
- entry crosses centre line L/R []
- entry too wide L/R []
- not entering with little finger L/R []
- other observations ....

Arm catch
It's all good apart from:
- excessive pause L/R []
- arm is too straight L/R []
- leading with the elbow L/R []
- feathering the catch L/R []
- palm cupped or fingers too open L/R []
- other observations ....

Arm pull
It's all good apart from:
- arm pull too wide L/R []
- arm pull is too narrow L/R []
- arm too straight/ deep L/R []
- feathering the water L/R []
- palms cupped L/R []
- fingers too open L/R []
- hand coming out of water L/R []
- hand clapping onto thigh L/R []
- other observations ....

Arm exit and recovery
It's all good apart from:
- pause on exit L/R []
- exit too short L/R []
- excess water being pulled up L/R []
- hand clapping on thigh L/R []
- recovery arm too wide L/R []
- recovery arm too bent L/R []
- recovery arm crossing centre L/R []
- recovery too slow L/R []
- other observations ....

Legs
It's all good apart from:
- unbalanced kick []
- weak kick []
- crossing feet []
- knees cycling []
- feet not flat []
- other observations ....

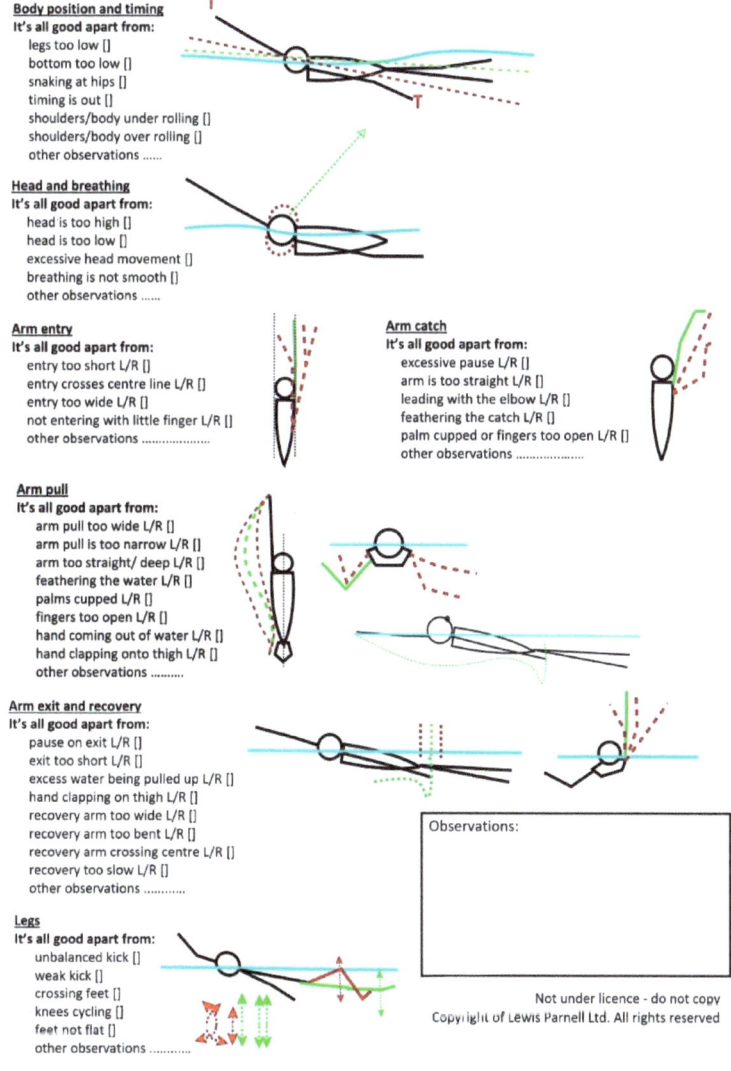

Observations:

Not under licence - do not copy
Copyright of Lewis Parnell Ltd. All rights reserved

Breast stroke

Body position and timing
It's all good apart from:
  Body position is too flat []
  pause in stroke []
  timing is out []
  other observations ....

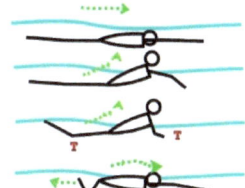

Head and breathing
It's all good apart from:
  excess head movement []
  head too far under water []
  limited head movement []
  breathing not smooth []
  other observations ....

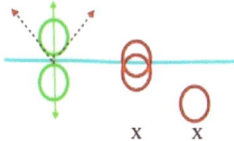

Arm pull
It's all good apart from:
  pull too far back []
  pull too narrow []
  pull too wide []
  slipping/feathering the water []
  arm too straight []
  elbow dropping []
  other observations ....

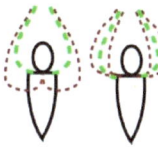 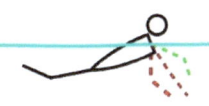

Leg kick
It's all good apart from:
  kick too wide []
  kick too narrow []
  dolphin kick between kicks []
  feet not turning out []
  flipper kick []
  screw kick []
  legs not snapping shut []
  knees dropping []
  other observations..........

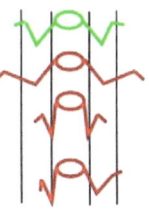 

Observations:

Not under licence - do not copy
Copyright of Lewis Parnell Ltd. All rights reserved

Butterfly

Body position and timing
It's all good apart from:
  legs too low []
  body too low []
  body motion too flat []
  body twisting []
  pause in stroke []
  timing is out []
  other observations .....

Head and breathing
It's all good apart from:
  head too high []
  head too far under water []
  chin not dropping to chest []
  excess head movement []
  breathing not smooth []
  breathing to one side []
  other observations ....

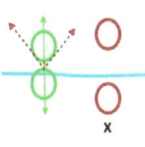

Arms entry
It's all good apart from:
  entry too short []
  'spoon' on entry []
  entry too narrow []
  entry too wide []
  uneven entry []
  not entering with thumb & finger []
  other observations ....

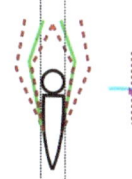
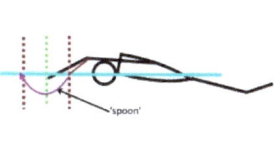

Catch
It's all good apart from:
  arms too straight/ deep []
  dropping elbows []
  excess pause []
  uneven arms []
  feathering water []
  palms cupped or fingers open []
  other observations ....

Arm pull
It's all good apart from:
  'S-curve' too big []
  arms uneven []
  arm pull too wide []
  arm crossing centre line []
  arm too straight/ deep []
  feathering the water []
  other observations ....

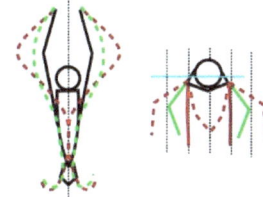

Arm exit and recovery
It's all good apart from:
  exit too short []
  exit too far back []
  exit not sweeping to side []
  pause on exit []
  arms too high on recovery []
  arms too bent on recovery []
  other observations ....

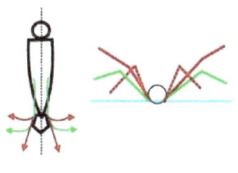

Observations:

Legs
It's all good apart from:
  breaststroke leg kick []
  knees moving apart []
  legs not staying together []
  excess bending of knees []
  weak kick []
  feet not flat []
  other observations ....

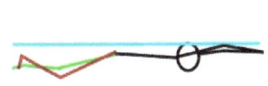

Not under licence - do not copy
Copyright of Lewis Parnell Ltd. All rights reserved

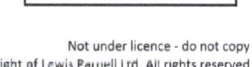

Section 2

The Detail

Faults

Causes

Corrections

FRONT CRAWL

1. <u>Overall front crawl theory</u>

The front crawl is as streamlined as possible with a gentle roll in the shoulders as each arm is recovered. All movement should be relaxed, controlled and never jerky. You should develop the rhythm of the stroke whilst really catching and holding onto the water throughout the pull.

You will see in the sections below that I give you the logical sequence of events in the stroke and the key timing point to check your stroke against. You will also see that I put great value on slowing the stroke down by using drills to enable you to concentrate on each individual element. I love catch-ups as these help you to work on individual parts of the stroke and reach the key timing point.

It's okay to concentrate on one part of the stroke at a time, either for a whole session or just one swim set. Once you have got that part of the stroke working well, you can practice and speed it up in your regular swimming. Your coaches will give you drill sets as well, but don't forget to use the warm-ups and swim-downs to practice technique. As you get tired during your sets and your stamina is flagging, make sure you concentrate on your technique – it will keep you moving well and will build the right muscles for that perfect stroke.

<u>Key drill set</u> – as I've said above, I really think catch-ups are a good drill for front crawl. There is a place for all of the other drills the coaches will give you, but catch-ups are the closest to the actual front crawl stroke. Catch-ups are really good for allowing you to concentrate on getting to the right timing position (the top swimmers often appear to be doing 'fast' catch-ups, especially the longer distance swimmers). Catch-ups get you to the key timing point easier. The key timing point is when the recovering arm is around halfway through the recovery as the pulling arm starts. It is beneficial to use flippers to provide you with the necessary balance and momentum through the water which enables you to concentrate on timings and each element of your catch, pull and recovery.

<u>Key flexibility bits</u> – shoulders, torso and ankles.

Shoulders. You'll need some good flexibility in your shoulders to swim great front crawl and it will help with keeping the recovery, entry and catch smooth. Mobility exercises such as swinging the arms in a controlled 'windmill' style are good - one arm at a time forward, one arm at a time backwards and then one arm forward and the other backwards at the same time. Once you have completed your work out and you are nicely warmed up (and not before - when your stretchy bits are cold) stretch the shoulders by placing your arm against a wall and gently rotating your body away.

It is also really useful to have a piece of rope with a series on knots in (for grip) to help flexibility in the shoulders. Hold the rope in a wide position for starters, with both hands in front of you and then move your (straight) arms back over your head holding onto the rope all the way back down to the back of your thighs, and then back to the front. Keep doing this over a period of time and reduce the distance between your hands. In the pool, you can increase shoulder flexibility by doing double arm backstroke but please note that excessive double arm backstroke use may cause shoulder soreness in some swimmers.

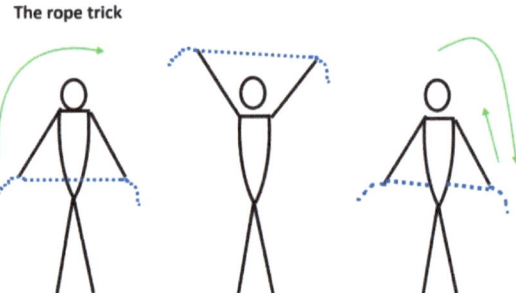

The rope trick

Torso. Good flexibility in the torso helps with the twist in the stroke so that you can get your arms in the most powerful position and easily recover your arms without upsetting the streamlining of the stroke. Stretching the back by touching your toes (either in a standing position or sat down) is very good. Sitting down touching your toes is also great for controlled stretching of the hamstrings. Remember, stretching should be controlled and you should be warmed up before doing it. You can also increase flexibility in your back by laying on your front and using your arms to lift the upper body, arching your back. Good twisting flexibility can be gained by lying on your back, soles of the feet on the floor with the knees bent. Allow your knees to rotate one side and then the other – gently twisting your back.

<u>Ankles</u>. Good flexibility within the ankles really allows you to get the best out of your kick as you get more of a range of movement. Simply taking the lower part of your foot in your hand and stretching it down will help. Sitting with your shins on the ground, legs under you with your feet flat under the bottom and moving your body backwards to stretch the ankles is another good flexibility exercise.

<u>Out of the water.</u> Anything you can do to improve general fitness and strength outside the pool will help you in the pool. The press is littered these days with examples of how swimmers are adding the 1% to their performance by lifting tractor tyres to pulling chains or even taking up ballet. I talk about 'feathering' in this guide as being one of the common technique faults. Feathering is where the arms zig-zag on the pull, slipping the water and this is due to a lack of strength in the muscles which are not able to keep hold of the water and push this past the body. It depends on your age as to what you should be doing in terms of fitness or strength building so I suggest you do your own research and take the advice of your coach.

It is good to understand the stroke position and it is generally easier to do this on dry land. It is particularly useful for swimmers to visualise the stroke and check the positions of the arms for example relative to the body at different parts of the stroke. Try to do this in the correct position where you can – either bending forward or ideally laying horizontally as you would be in the water.

2. <u>Body position and timing</u>

The body should be almost flat with the legs being slightly lower in the water than the top half of your body. Your shoulders will rotate gently side to side and the torso will twist nicely with every arm stroke as the shoulder of the recovering arm is higher than the shoulder of the arm doing the pulling. Slight rolling and twisting makes the recovery much easier and reduces the amount the head needs to turn to breathe. The torso twists so that your bottom can remain as still as possible to maximise streamlining and keep your legs in a good kicking position. Your legs will supply the balance and some of the power.

The key timing point as displayed by top front crawl swimmers is detailed in the diagram above at the 'T' points. The recovering arm is around halfway through the recovery before the pulling arm starts the catch. Correct timing provides a good rhythm, a balanced stroke and allows the pulling arm time to prepare for the catch.

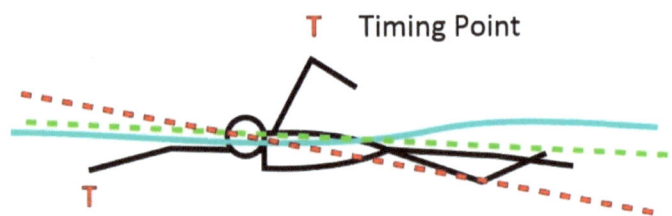

Issue	Likely cause	Remedy	Drills	Out of the water
Timing is out (rushes catch and upsets stroke).	There is a pause elsewhere in the stroke.	Identify where the fault is and correct.	Catch-ups. See 'Key drill set' above for detail.	Practice on dry land to get to key timing point.
	Entry hand goes straight into pull, missing the catch.	Break the entry to catch motion with a short pause.	See 'Key drill set' above.	Practice on dry land to enable catch.
	Incorrect arm pull - speeds up stroke into a windmill.	Correct arm pull.	Catch-ups with flippers - focus on correct position.	Run through correct position on dry land.
Legs too low in the water (causes drag and slows you down).	The head position is too high.	Ensure water line is just above the hair-line.	Change the head position during training.	Look at the position of other swimmers.
	Legs aren't effective (either weak kick or rate is too slow).	Increase the leg kick rate and increase range of kick.	Practice legs only to build up strength.	Build leg strength with exercise. Increase flexibility in the ankles.
The body is snaking with movement from side to side around	Excessive head movement, generally and during	Alter head position If necessary and control during	Breathe every 5 strokes and control head.	Run through head movement during

hips (slows and unbalances).	breathing.	breathing.	Correct breathing.	breathing on dry land.
	The hand entry or arm pull is crossing the centre line.	Correct hand entry position and keep arm pull in line with the side of the body.	Imagine you are swimming above a brick wall – the arms need to stay each side of the wall.	Check arm position when you pull yourself out of the water, that will be the strongest position.

3. Head

Your face is in the water during front crawl with your eyes looking at a point 5 to 10 metres in front of you. The waterline should be somewhere just above your hairline. The head needs to be controlled and should not move excessively or in jerky movements as this will upset the streamline. Think of the head as a heavy bowling ball – where your head goes; the body is likely to follow. You wouldn't walk along the street wobbling your head all over the place!

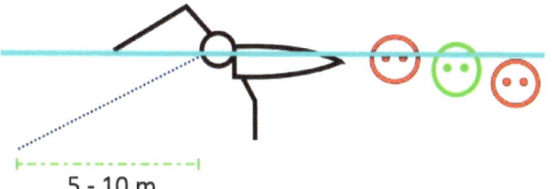

5 - 10 m

Issue	Likely cause	Remedy	Drills	Out of the water
Head is too high (causes other end of body to sink) or is too low (causes drag and interferes with arm recovery).	Wrong positioning of the head – not looking 5 – 10m in front.	Alter the head position, feel the water on the correct position (take your cap off as it will make this easier).	Slow the stroke down by doing catch-ups. Then concentrate on the head position.	Look at the head position of other swimmers.
Excess head movement (causes drag, upsets timing and streamlining).	Excess movement in other areas of the stroke (e.g. arms crossing the centre point in the pull; wide swinging recovery).	Check the other parts of the stroke against the diagrams and correct.	Slow the stroke down by doing catch-ups. Then concentrate on controlling the head.	Run through the correct positions of the stroke on dry land.

| | Lack of control or concentration. | Fix the head position as if was an extension of the spine. Practice. | Slow the stroke down by doing catch-ups. Then concentrate on controlling the head position. | Try walking along moving the head excessively and see what effect this has on the body. |

4. <u>Breathing</u>

You breathe by turning the head to the side of the recovering arm. The movement doesn't need to be great because, as you move through the water, you will create a bow wave of water which you can breathe into. Coaches will generally ask swimmers to breathe out steadily through the nose when your face is back in the water as this 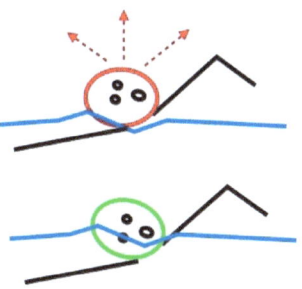 helps to control the stroke and stops water going up the nose. I like to hold onto the breath and only blow it out when I am about to take another breath. This means I can benefit from holding onto the oxygen in my lungs for longer and I'm not gasping before the next stroke. I blow all the air out of my nose, first as a trickle (to stop water going up) and then in one big explosion before the next breath.

Swimmers are routinely taught to breathe bilaterally (every third arm recovery, alternating the sides for breathing). Breathing bilaterally balances the stroke and you can teach yourself to do this and be comfortable in doing so. Longer distance swimmers may wish to breathe on the same side to get the necessary oxygen and also to create and settle into their rhythm (it can be jolly difficult to maintain bilateral breathing over longer periods). By contrast, sprinters are likely to breathe less as keeping the stroke going without pausing for a breath can be quicker. You will probably need to do a mix of breathing during training so you are well practiced for your race.

Issue	Likely cause	Remedy	Drills	Out of the water
Head turning too much - looking at the ceiling, behind or too far forward; or a combination of these (unbalances the body, affects streamlining and can cause snaking).	Excess movement in other areas of the stroke (e.g. arms crossing the centre point in the pull; body rolling too much).	Check the other parts of the stroke against the diagrams and rectify. Keep all movements controlled.	Slow the stroke down by doing catch-ups. Then concentrate on the breathing position and action.	Try walking along moving the head excessively and see what effect this has on the body. Practice motion on land.
	A lack of concentration or control allowing head to turn too much.	Limit the head to smaller movements. Pick a level on the side of the pool to look at when breathing.	Slow the stroke down by doing catch-ups. Then concentrate on breathing into the bow wave.	Spot a level on the poolside to focus on when breathing (coaches knees are about the right height).
Long breath (causes a pause in arm pull and affects timing).	There is a pause elsewhere in the stroke or the arm pull is too deep which delays recovery.	Check other parts of the stroke and identify pause. Speed up the recovery arm.	Slow the stroke down by doing catch-ups. Try to return the face to the water quicker.	Look at the breathing action of other swimmers. Practice action on dry land.

| Jerky breathing/ gasping for air in a rush/ long breath (upsets the stroke). | Exhaling too quickly or exhaling through the mouth. | Hold onto the air in your lungs until just before breathing again. Exhale through nose. | Concentrate on holding and releasing the air from your lungs, inhale mouth – exhale nose. | Try the timing of releasing the air on dry land. |

5. **Arms entry**

Whilst one arm is pulling the water, the other arm is recovering and getting ready to enter the water. Your first finger and thumb should enter the water first and your hand should be slightly tilted to reduce any resistance. 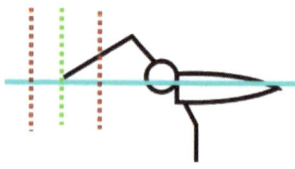 Your hand should then stretch forward just under the surface of the water where it pauses momentarily, getting into the correct position ready to start the catch.

The entry point needs to be in the right place to start off the pull in the strongest possible position and this should be in line with your shoulder. Too wide or too narrow will almost certainly lead to snaking of the body at the hips. Check the diagram to see the point your hand should be entering both in terms of distance and direction from your shoulder.

Issue	Likely cause	Remedy	Drills	Out of the water
Entry too short (misses out on part of the catch and pull).	The stroke is being rushed. The pull of the other arm is too far advanced causing the entry arm to catch up.	Correct entry point and push your hand forward and take a short pause before the catch. Check key timing point.	Catch-ups, making sure the hand entry position is level with the wrist of the outstretched arm.	Complete motion on dry land. Look at the arm entry position of other swimmers who have a smooth stroke.
Entry too long (can cause slapping of hands, snaking of hips and incorrect position for hand to start catch).	Over-reaching on entry or the recovery arm may be too straight.	Shorten entry to correct point and ensure the recovering arm is suitably bent with a high elbow on entry.	Catch-ups, making sure the hand entry position is level with the wrist of the outstretched arm.	Complete catch-up motion on dry land, making sure entry is level with the wrist of the outstretched arm.
Entry too narrow (crossing the centre line will unbalance body, cause snaking and an over-turn of head in breathing).	The recovery arm is swinging too far across to the centre line or you are over-rolling or over-breathing.	Correct hand entry position, any over roll or over breathing. Push hand forward on entry in line with shoulder.	Slow the stroke down by doing catch-ups. Then concentrate on hand entry position and keeping the body flatter.	Practice motion of entry and pushing forward in line with shoulder, keeping the body flatter.

Entry too wide (arms not in the most powerful position).	You are not bringing your arms over enough or the head is being buried in the water.	Correct hand entry position so it enters in line with your shoulder. Correct head position.	Slow the stroke down by doing catch-ups. Then concentrate on hand entry position.	Practice motion of entry and pushing forward in line with shoulder.

6. **Catch**

From the outstretched arm position in front of you, the palm of the hand and fingers turns down just over 45 degrees. This is called catching the water and it is important to get hold of as much of the water at this point to give you the best forward leverage. The forearm moves down next and the elbow stays in a high position where it is. This presents the largest possible amount of your hand and forearm to the water at this point in the stroke. When the hand and forearm are almost 90 degrees to the upper part of the arm, the whole arm starts to move backwards on the pull through.

Issue	Likely cause	Remedy	Drills	Out of the water
No catch – straight arm (is difficult, loses the water and can cause shoulder problems).	Not moving the hand first, then the forearm and maintaining the high position of the elbow.	Concentrate on the stages of movement – hand first, then forearm. Keep the elbow high and still.	Slow the stroke down with catch-ups. Follow the sequence in order – hand, then forearm, then elbow.	Run through sequence on dry land – hand, forearm, elbow high and still. Build up the forearm muscles.
No catch – dropped elbow (loses the water and power).	Incorrectly, the elbow is the first thing to move backwards and leads the pull.	Concentrate on the stages – hand first, then forearm. Keep the elbow high and still.	Catch-ups, keep the elbow high and still. Make sure the hand and forearm move first.	Check your elbow position as you pull up out of the pool – notice it stays in the same position.

Excess pause before catch - arm stays extended for too long (upsets rhythm of stroke).	The outstretched arm is likely to be waiting for the pulling arm to catch up.	Correct timing. Check pull for any faults or pauses and correct. Speed up pull motion.	Do catch-ups and start to speed up the stroke until the key timing point is reached.	Time the pause of other swimmers. Run through timing on dry land.
	There may be too many leg kicks for the cycle of the arm pull.	Reduce the number of leg kicks per arm cycle.	Normal swim, counting and then reducing leg kick rate.	Count the leg kick rate of other swimmers.
Feathering catch - hand and arm zig-zag in water (slips the water).	Lack of strength in the wrist or arm. Excessive rolling of the body, possibly caused by excessive head movement.	Check the body is not over-rolling or head is moving excessively. Control catch as far as possible, keeping to correct position.	Catch ups with flippers. Regulate head movement. Concentrate on keeping to the S-curve; it will be difficult at first.	Build up wrist, forearm and arm strength by exercise.
	The palm of the hand is cupped or the fingers are open too wide.	Flatten palm / close fingers (a little gap between the fingers is okay).	One arm only, concentrating on the hand and finger position.	Practice sculling the water and feeling the position with the most resistance.

7. <u>Arm pull</u>

The pull and the push should follow an S-curve and if you were to look at yourself from above, the pull and push happens at the side of the body and not underneath your chest or stomach. A common fault is pulling over the centre line and this can cause many problems elsewhere in the stroke. A handy reminder is to think that you are swimming along the top of a wall and your hands cannot cross the wall.

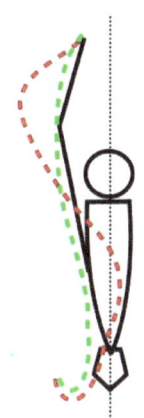

The first part of the pull should be slightly slower than the push as this enables you to get a good hold of the water.

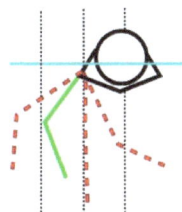

The remaining pull and the push is faster and this is where you have the most power. It is important to keep feeling the water on the pull and push in practice to check you are maximising the power. An easy way of checking where your power lies is to look at your arm position when you pull yourself up out of the pool. It is difficult to get yourself out when your arms are too straight, too narrow or too wide.

Issue	Likely cause	Remedy	Drills	Out of the water
Pull too wide (loss of power).	Incorrect hand entry position and pull through.	Correct entry in line with shoulder and pull to follow S-curve in line with side of body.	Catch-ups, concentrate on pull. Look above the water to check entry point.	Check the position of your arms as you pull yourself out of the water.
Pull too narrow or crosses over (loss of power, will cause snaking and over-rolling of body).	Incorrect hand entry position and pull through. Excessive roll possibly due to over-breathing.	Correct entry in line with shoulder and pull to follow the S-curve in line with the side of your body.	Think you are swimming along an imaginary wall which your hands cannot cross.	Check the position of your arms as you pull yourself out of the water.
S-curve too big/ exaggerated (you will lose the water).	Incorrect action. Weak arm muscles. Excessive roll possibly due to over breathing.	Ensure the pull follows line of the side of your body and correct any over-rolling or over-breathing.	Catch ups, concentrating on keeping the body flat and pull in correct position.	Practice positions and action on dry land. Build strength of arms.
Feathering - hand and arm zig-zag (slips the water).	Lack of arm strength, excessive rolling of the body or excessive head movement.	Check the body is not over-rolling and head is not moving excessively. Control pull.	Control roll & head movement. Concentrate on keeping to the S-curve; it'll be difficult at first.	Build up arm strength by exercise.

	The palm of the hand is cupped or the fingers are open too wide.	Flatten palm/ close fingers (a little gap in the fingers is okay).	One arm only, concentrating on the hand and finger position.	Practice sculling the water and feel the position with the most resistance.
Pull too deep - arms too straight (loss of power and can be very difficult to do).	Not keeping to sequence - hand, then forearm, elbow high and still).	Keep to sequence, keep elbow high. Ensure correct bend in elbow.	Catch-ups, keeping the elbow high and still concentrate on sequence.	Check the position of your arms as you pull yourself out of the water.

8. Arm exit and recovery

The push through should end on the upper thigh with the palm making a final push backwards to maximise power. The hand comes out to the side to start the recovery rather than 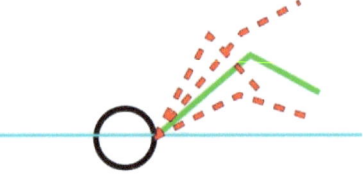 straight up which will cause a pause and excess drag. The lower arm and the hand should be relaxed during recovery and should hang down from the elbow around half way between the elbow and the water. The torso will twist nicely and the body will rotate just enough to allow the arm to be recovered easily and quickly. Recovering your arms too straight, too bent or too high will upset your stroke and waste valuable energy and time.

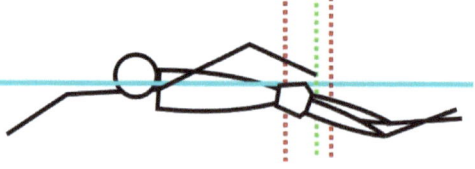

Issue	Likely cause	Remedy	Drills	Out of the water
Exit too short (missing out on the vital power push at the end).	Rushing the stroke and or a lack of power in the arms.	Mark the point of exit on the upper thigh and brush your thumb on your leg to check.	Normal swimming or catch-ups, concentrate on exiting at the desired position.	Exercises to increase arm strength. Mark exit point on your thigh.
Exit too long (overstretching causes a pause).	Incorrect exit point. Hand is not sweeping out to the side at the end of the push.	Brush thumb on upper thigh to check exit point. Exit to the side, not straight up.	Normal swimming or catch-ups, concentrate on exiting at the desired position.	Watch other swimmers' exit points. Practice on dry land.
Pause on exit - hand seems to hang around in the water before exit (upsets rhythm).	The catch has started too early on the other arm leaving the body unbalanced forward.	Pause hand on entry with a nice stretch forward. Check key timing point.	Slow stroke with catch-ups and gradually speed up until key timing point has been reached.	Watch other swimmers and check their timing points. Practice timing on dry land.
Recovery arm too high (will unbalance the stroke and takes longer to recover to entry).	Incorrect recovery arm position. The pull arm may be crossing over under the body.	Rectify pull arm position (see pull section). Reposition recovery arm.	Bend elbow and drag fingertips across water surface during recovery.	Watch other swimmers. Practice swimming through an imaginary tube.

Recovery arm too straight (upsets smoothness and can cause snaking).	Incorrect recovery arm position. The pull arm may be crossing over under the body.	Rectify pull arm position (see pull section). Reposition recovery arm.	Bend elbow and drag fingertips across water surface during recovery.	Practice swimming through an imaginary tube. Increase flexibility in the shoulders.
Recovery arm too bent (loss of counter balance to the pulling arm).	Incorrect arm positioning.	Reposition recovery arm.	Slow stroke down with catch ups and widen recovery position.	Watch other swimmers' arm position.

9. Legs

The legs move alternately, with one leg kicking downward while the other leg kicks upward. The legs are important to stabilize the body position and provide forward propulsion. Longer distance swimmers will generally use their legs less (4 kicks per arm cycle or even 2) as they soak up the oxygen quickly. Sprinters maximise their legs (6 or 8 kicks per arm cycle) and they are an important part of the stroke in contributing to the overall speed. The usual kicks per arm cycle will be 4 or 6.

You should be kicking your feet from the knee (in the same way you would kick a football) with the thigh remaining fairly static and providing the muscular power. The main power of the kick comes from the lower leg and the foot which is driven by the thigh muscles. Your ankles should be flexible with the toes pointing backwards. Keep the feet in the water as much as possible – kicking air won't help you along.

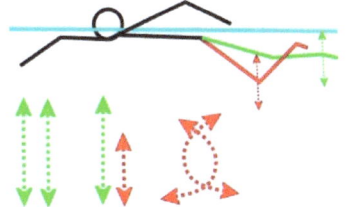

Issue	Likely cause	Remedy	Drills	Out of the water
Crossing feet - usually with one always being on the top (unbalances stroke).	Unbalanced stroke, usually caused by breathing to one side or pull across the centre line.	Bilateral breathing. Control any over rolling in the body and check pull position.	Bilateral breathing on 3, 5 or 7 arm cycles. Leg kick only to build strength.	Build up general leg strength.
One foot kicking more than the other - acts as a rudder (loss of power).	Stroke is not balanced, usually caused by breathing to one side.	Bilateral breathing. Concentrate on even leg kick.	Bilateral breathing on 3, 5 or 7 arm cycles. Leg kick only to build strength.	Build up general leg strength.

The 'plonk' kick - one leg does an almighty kick which makes a plonking sound.	There is a pause in stroke or the pull arm is crossing centre line (the leg kick compensates).	Correct and control stroke and check key timing point for any pauses.	Bilateral breathing on 3, 5 or 7 arm cycles. Restart stroke using catch ups and flippers.	Build up general leg strength. Increase flexibility of ankles.
Cycling - excess bending of the knees leads to a pedalling motion (ineffective and causes drag).	Kicking from the knee and not using the thigh effectively.	Keep the leg and knee straighter and utilise thigh muscles. Practice a football kicking motion.	Leg kick only to build strength. Leg kick in backstroke position - keep knees in water.	Build up leg strength. Increase ankle flexibility. Practice 'ball kick' position.
Weak kick (doesn't provide power to the stroke).	Weak leg muscles and incorrect technique.	Increase leg kick rate per stroke. Increase the kick motion from the thigh muscles.	Leg kick only to build strength.	Build up general leg strength. Increase flexibility of ankles.
Feet at 90 degrees (causes drag).	Lack of ankle flexibility. Incorrect position of feet.	Point toes away from body.	Leg kick to concentrate on foot position.	Increase flexibility of ankles.

Case study

Joshua. I started by completing the front crawl stroke card so I could show Joshua where his stroke was good and where the action did not meet the accepted position.

Joshua had excessive head movement with one leg kicking more than the other and his stroke was untidy and rushed. Joshua was over-turning the head to breath and was moving his head around whilst his face was in the water.

I could see that the excessive head movement and erratic leg kick were being caused by the arm pull crossing a long way over the centre line. I thought it would be useful for Joshua to understand what was happening to his body position when his head moved around too much so I asked him to walk along the poolside and rock his head around. He was surprised how this affected the rest of his body and in particular the upper half. I then asked him to walk normally and to check what his head was doing. Naturally, his head was remaining still and his body remained in line.

I explained what the overall stoke action should look like so he could keep this in mind as I changed the other parts of the stroke. I located the point where the water should be on Joshua's forehead and once he marked this himself, he swam a few lengths to feel where the water should be. Taking his swim cap off made it easier to feel the water.

He then practiced breathing smoothly by only turning his head a little and trying to breathe into the bow wave. Amazingly for a senior swimmer he hadn't heard of the bow wave and how this could be utilised to streamline the stroke. I asked him to turn his head only enough so that he could see my knees - he told me he could regularly see what was happening in the balcony when he swam front crawl.

Looking from the front on, I could see that both arms were pulling across the centre line with one arm (the one when he took a breath) crossing more than the other. This was causing the stroke to be unbalanced and was causing excess rolling. Because the pulling arm was taking longer as it was going further over the centreline during the breath, it was causing the head to roll forward to force the same arm to catch up when it was being recovered. Also by pulling over the centre line it was causing the hips to snake to compensate for the over-balance which was causing drag and another head movement to compensate the sideways movement in the body.

I asked Joshua to pull himself out of the water and hold his arm position half way up. The arms go to the natural power point – the position at which the arms provide the most power. If the arms are too wide; you have limited power and can't haul yourself out, too narrow; it is more difficult and you are unbalanced. It's a great way of showing swimmers where their power point is and the relative position of the hands and arms to their body. It's particularly useful for swimmers with straight arm pulls and it is incredibly difficult to lift yourself out of the pool with straight arms.

Joshua concentrated on widening the entry point in line with his shoulders so he started off in the right position. He raised his head up out of the water a little every five or so strokes so he could watch the entry position. I then got him to imagine he was swimming just above an imaginary brick wall with the wall being 30 centimetres wide and stopping about 20 centimetres below his chest. His arm pull could therefore not go across that brick wall. This is a handy thought, as I now often call to him 'brick wall' and he knows what I'm talking about. This widened his stroke. We also did some bi-lateral breathing to balance the stroke out but kept this to a drill mainly as Joshua's fastest racing style is to breathe to one side.

To tidy up the stroke we concentrated on having more of a glide to each arm at the start of the catch using catch-ups as a drill. The uneven leg kick corrected itself in the main from the changes in the arm pull however the legs still remained weaker when compared to the arms so he had to do more kick to increase his strength.

We returned to repositioning the head and controlling the breathing after the other corrections were made.

BACKSTROKE

1. Overall backstroke theory

In backstroke, you lie flat on your back and the arms alternate so one arm is underwater while the other arm is recovering. The theory is that the backstroke is as streamlined as possible with a gentle roll of the shoulders to enable the pulling arm to get into the correct power position and the recovering arm to recover easily. All movements should be controlled and you should try and develop the rhythm of the stroke whilst really catching and holding onto the water throughout the pull. Whilst the arms provide most of the power, the legs provide balance and contribute to the forward momentum.

You will note in the sections below that I give you the logical sequence of events in the stroke and the key timing point against which to check your stroke. It's okay to concentrate on one part of the stroke at a time, either for a whole session or just one swim set. Once you have got that part of the stroke working well, you can practice and speed it up in your regular swimming. Your coaches will give you drill sets, but don't forget to use the warm-ups and swim-downs to practice your technique. As you get tired during your sets and your stamina is flagging, make sure you concentrate on your technique – it will keep you moving well and will build the right muscles for that perfect stroke.

Key drill set – The best drill for backstroke is moving one arm only at a time with the other at the side of the body; hand pressed against the thigh. This enables you to concentrate on the recovery, roll and arm pull and it is the closest thing to the actual stroke. You can also try this using alternate arms as catch-ups, but you should wait until the pulling arm has come back to the thigh before staring the other arm off. The use of flippers is good as they provide you with the necessary momentum through the water and the balance to enable you to concentrate on timings and each element of your catch, pull and recovery. Double arm backstroke (or old English backstroke) is good for concentrating on the recovery position and the push part of the stroke – it doesn't however allow you to roll to one side to perfect the catch and the pull.

Key flexibility bits – shoulders, torso and ankles.

Shoulders. You'll need some good flexibility in the shoulders to swim great backstroke as it will keep the rolling smooth and enable you to get the arm into the best power position without upsetting the streamlining of your stroke. Mobility exercises such as swinging the arms in a controlled 'windmill' style are good - one arm at a time forward, one arm at a time backwards and then one arm forward and the other backwards at the same time. Once you have completed your work out and you are nicely warmed up (and not before when your flexi bits are cold) stretch the shoulders by placing your arm against a wall and gently rotate your body away.

It is also really useful to have a piece of rope with a series on knots in to help flexibility in the shoulders. Hold the rope in a wide position for starters, with both hands in front of you and then move your (straight) arms back over your head holding onto the rope all the way back down to the back of your thighs, and then back to the front. Keep doing this over a period of time and reduce the distance between your hands. In the pool, you can increase shoulder flexibility by doing double arm backstroke but please note that excessive double arm backstroke can cause shoulder soreness in some swimmers.

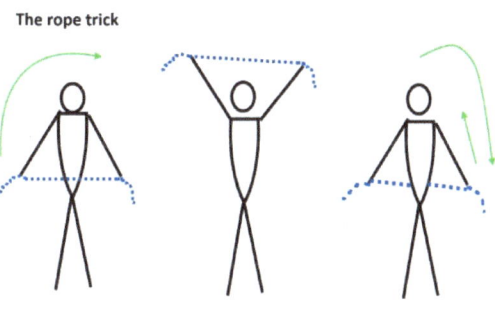
The rope trick

Torso. Good flexibility helps with the twist in the stroke so that your arms can get to the most powerful position and easily recover your arms without upsetting the streamlining of the stroke. Stretching the back by touching your toes (either in a standing position or sat down) is very good. Sitting down doing this is also great for the hamstrings. Remember, stretching should be controlled and you should be warmed up before doing it. You can also increase flexibility in your back by laying on your front and using your arms to lift the upper body, arching your back. Good twisting flexibility can be gained by lying on your back, soles of the feet on the floor with the knees bent. Allow your knees to rotate one side and then the other – gently twisting your back.

Ankles. Good flexibility within the ankles really allows you to get the best out of your kick as you get more of a range of movement. Simply taking the lower part of your foot in your hand and stretching it down will help. Sitting with your shins on the ground, legs under you with your feet flat under the bottom and moving your body backwards to stretch the ankles is another good flexibility exercise.

Out of the water. Anything you can do to improve general fitness and strength outside the pool will help you in the pool. The press is littered these days with examples of how swimmers are adding the 1% to their performance by lifting tractor tyres to pulling chains or even taking up ballet. I talk about 'feathering' in this guide as being one of the common technique faults. Feathering is where the arms zig-zag on the pull, slipping the water and this is due to a lack of strength in the muscles which are not able to keep hold of the water and push this past the body. It depends on your age as to what you should be doing in terms of fitness or strength building so I suggest you do your own research and take the advice of your coach.

It is good to understand the stroke position and it is generally easier to do this on dry land. It is particularly useful for swimmers to visualise the stroke and check the positions of the arms for example relative to the body at different parts of the stroke. Try to do this in the correct position where you can – laying horizontally on your back as you would be in the water.

2. <u>Body position and timing</u>

Your body should be almost flat in the water with your legs being slightly lower than the top half of your body. Your body will rotate gently and the torso will twist nicely with every arm stroke as the shoulder of the recovering arm is higher than the shoulder of the arm doing the pulling. The shoulders roll more than the torso to enable you to get the right position of the pulling arm.   Your body should remain streamlined and not move from side to side at the hips. You legs will supply the balance.

The key timing point displayed by top backstroke swimmers is detailed in the diagram with the recovering arm just preparing to enter the water as the pulling arm is completing the push down at the end of the stroke. This helps provide the forward momentum at the point the recovery arm is entering the water and then allows you to start the roll to the other side to start the catch.

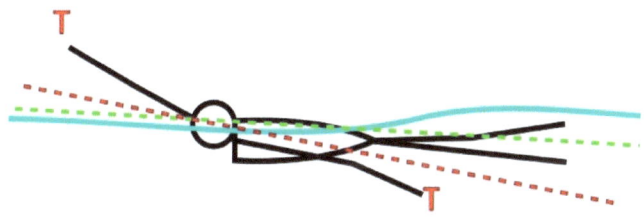

Issue	Likely cause	Remedy	Drills	Out of the water
Timing is out (upsets the rhythm of the stroke and slows you down).	Pauses in stroke and incorrect arm pull.	Correct faults in the stroke.	Backstroke with flippers, concentrating on the key timing position.	Practice arm motion on dry land to get key timing point correct.
Legs too low in the water (causes drag and slows you down).	The head position is too high.	Check and alter the head position.	Change the head position during training.	Look at the position of other swimmers.
	The legs aren't kicking enough (either leg kick rate is too slow or not at all).	Increase the leg kick rate and range and make sure the legs are effective.	Do more practice with the legs only to build strength.	Do leg exercises to build strength.
	The bottom is sat too deep in the water with the body bent.	Push the waist up closer to the top of the water.	Backstroke catch-ups and concentrate on raising the waist.	Build core body strength.
The body is snaking - movement from side to side around hips (slows and unbalances).	The head is moving around too much.	Check and alter the head position.	Practice keeping the head still during training, concentrating on a point on the ceiling.	Walk along and move your head about – see what effect this has on the rest of your body.

	The arm pull may be too far away from the body and the arms are likely to be too straight.	Make sure the shoulders are rolling and bend the elbow to reach the correct position.	Backstroke catch-ups with flippers concentrating on the roll and position of the arms.	Check your arm position on dry land and where this needs to be in relation to your body.
The body stays too flat and the shoulders are not rotating to aid arm pull (hinders recovery & pull).	The arm pull may be too far away from the body and the arms are likely to be too straight.	Make sure the shoulders are rolling enough and bend the elbow to reach the correct position.	Backstroke catch-ups with flippers concentrating on the roll and position of the arms.	Check your arm position on dry land and where this needs to be in relation to your body.
The body is over-rolling (causes pauses and unbalances stroke).	The arm pull may be too deep.	Restrict the rolling shoulder movement and reposition the arm pull.	Backstroke catch-ups with flippers concentrating on the roll and position of the pull arm.	Check your arm position on dry land and where this needs to be in relation to your body.
	The head may be moving excessively.	Restrict the head movement.	Imagine trying to keep a cup full of water balanced on the forehead.	Walk along and move your head about – see what effect this has on the rest of your body.

10. <u>Head and breathing</u>

Your face will be out of the water with your eyes looking up at the ceiling at a point slightly behind your feet. The waterline will be at the top of your head, somewhere between your crown and the hairline on your forehead. The head needs to be controlled and should not move excessively or in jerky movements. Think of the head as a heavy bowling ball – where your head goes, the body is likely to follow. You wouldn't walk along the street wobbling your head all over the place!

To control the breathing and build a rhythm in the stroke, you should breathe in through the mouth during the recovery of one arm and breathe out through the mouth and nose during the push phase of the same arm. Breathing out through the nose helps stop water going up the nostrils. Some swimmers find it easier to breathe every other stroke.

Issue	Likely cause	Remedy	Drills	Out of the water
Head is too high (causes legs to sink) or is too low (causes drag and interferes with arm recovery).	Wrong positioning of the head.	Check and alter the head position. Locate the point where the water should be and try to feel this when swimming.	Do backstroke kick with flippers, arms down by your side to locate and feel the correct position.	Look at the position of other swimmers.
Excess head movement (causes drag and upsets timing and streamlining).	Excess movement in other areas of the stroke (e.g. recovering arm crossing the centre	Check the other parts of the stroke against the stroke card diagrams and	Slow the stroke down by doing backstroke catch-ups. Then concentrate	Look at the position of other swimmers.

		point; pull too wide or too deep.	rectify.	on the head position.	
		May just be lack of concentration and practice.	Fix the head position and try to balance an imaginary cup of water on your forehead. Practice.	Slow the stroke down by doing catch-ups. Then concentrate on the head position.	Try walking along moving the head excessively and see what effect this has on the body.
Erratic breathing, gasping for breath (causes pauses and upsets rhythm).	Lack of control of breathing timing, holding onto breath for several strokes.	Practice breathing in (mouth) on the recovery and out (nose) on the pull phase during each stroke cycle.	Use flippers to provide the forward momentum and slow the stroke to practice the breathing.	Practice timing out of the water.	

11. Arms entry

Whilst one arm is pulling the water, the other arm is recovering and preparing to enter the water. The little finger enters the water first to reduce any resistance to the hand entry. The entry point needs to be in the right place to start off the pull in the best possible way and should be in line with your shoulder. The arm should be kept straight on entry.

Issue	Likely cause	Remedy	Drills	Out of the water
Entry too short (means missing out on part of catch and pull).	The recovery arm is not straight.	Practice keeping the arm straight and the elbow locked straight.	Backstroke catch-ups with flippers to isolate and correct positioning.	Practice the stroke on dry land. Watch other swimmers.
Entry crosses the centre line (will unbalance stroke and cause snaking).	The recovery arm is not straight.	Practice keeping the arm straight and the elbow locked straight.	Backstroke catch-ups with flippers to isolate and correct positioning.	Practice the stroke on dry land. Watch other swimmers.
	The pulling arm is too deep or is too straight.	Reposition the pulling arm position.	Backstroke one arm with flippers to isolate and correct positioning.	Practice the stroke on dry land. Watch other swimmers.
	The shoulders are over rolling.	Control the rolling.	Backstroke one arm with flippers and control the rolling.	Practice roll position on dry land.

Entry too wide (missing the catch and arms not in the most powerful position).	Not bringing the arms over in a straight line from exit point to entry point.	Watch your arm as it recovers and ensure it is in line with the shoulder.	Backstroke catch-ups with flippers to isolate and correct positioning.	Practice the stroke on dry land. Watch other swimmers.

12. <u>Catch</u>

From the outstretched arm entry position, the arm sinks slightly lower than the shoulder to provide leverage and the palm of the hand and fingers turns out just over 45 degrees. This is called catching the water and it is important to catch as much of the water at this point to give you the best advantage. The forearm moves out next and the elbow drops as your shoulder lowers in the water from the roll – this gives you the greatest surface area of your arm pulling the water at this point in the stroke and a nice bent arm to get you into the power position. Note: the elbow drops downwards towards the bottom of the pool – it does not lead the pull through.

Issue	Likely cause	Remedy	Drills	Out of the water
No catch – straight arm (is difficult, loses the water and causes snaking).	Lack of roll in the shoulders and no bend in the elbow.	Keep to sequence – hand first, then forearm. Make sure the elbow is bent.	One arm with flippers to isolate and correct positioning and sequence.	Run through the sequence and position on dry land. Build up the forearm muscles.
No catch – leading with the elbow (losing the water and losing the power).	Incorrectly, the elbow is the first thing to move and leads the hand and forearm.	Keep to sequence – hand first, then forearm. Make sure the elbow is bent but level with the hand.	One arm with flippers to isolate and correct positioning and sequence.	Run through the sequence and position on dry land.

Excess pause before catch - arm stays extended for too long (loss of forward momentum).	The catch arm is waiting for the pull arm.	Speed up arm pull.	Use flippers to correct timing and speed up arm pull.	Run through the sequence and position on dry land.
	There is a pause on push or exit of other hand.	Lack of a final push down or incorrect hand position on push (hand clamps onto thigh).	Backstroke one arm with flippers to correct arm push and exit positions.	Run through the sequence and position on dry land.
	There is not enough roll to help lift the shoulder and other arm out of the water.	Increase the roll.	Use flippers to provide forward momentum and ensure roll is sufficient.	Run through the sequence and position on dry land.
	There may be too many leg kicks within the cycle.	Change the leg kick cycle to two less kicks per arm cycle, it will be difficult at first.	Count and then reduce the kicks per arm cycle until pause rectified.	Watch and count other swimmers leg kick to arm cycles.
Feathering catch - hand and arm zig-zag (slips the water).	Lack of strength in the arm.	Will improve with more backstroke swimming.	Arms only to build up strength.	Build up bicep and forearm strength by exercise.

	Too flat will put pressure on arm; over-roll will cause excessive movements in arm.	Check the body and shoulders are rolling just enough to allow the pull arm to be in the power position.	Use flippers to provide the support and power and concentrate on correct roll position.	Run through the sequence and position on dry land.
	The palm of the hand is cupped or the fingers are open too wide.	Flatten palm / close fingers (a little gap between the fingers is okay).	One arm only, concentrating on the hand and finger position.	Practice sculling the water and feeling the position with the most resistance.

13. Arm pull

During the pull phase, your hand follows a downwards and outwards semi-circular path from the catch to the side of the hip (see diagrams). Your palm and forearm face away from your swimming direction and the elbow always points downward towards the bottom of the pool so the arm can push the maximum amount of water backward in order to push your body forward.

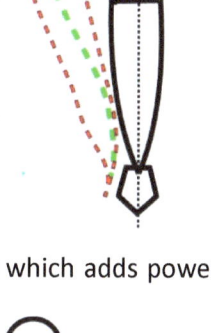

The push phase consists of pushing the palm of your hand towards your feet with the fingers pointing upward. Again, the goal is to push your body forward against the water. At the very end of the push, the palm flaps down to a depth of around 35 centimetres which adds power to the push and helps raise the shoulder in preparation for the recovery. During the pull and the push, the fingers of the hand can be slightly apart as this will increase the resistance of the hand in the water.

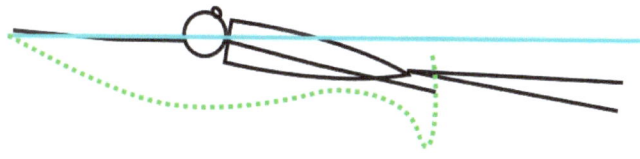

Issue	Likely cause	Remedy	Drills	Out of the water
Pull too wide (loss of power and can cause snaking of the hips).	Hand entry position is too wide.	Reposition in line with your shoulder.	One arm, concentrating on hand entry position.	Run through the entry position on dry land.
	The arm is too straight.	Bend the elbow more and bring hand in closer to body.	One arm, concentrating on the roll and elbow position.	Run through position on dry land.
	The shoulders are not rolling enough.	Rotate the shoulders more.	One arm, concentrating on the roll and elbow position.	Run through roll positions on dry land.
Pull too narrow – hand is too close to the body).	Excessive roll and/ or elbow is too bent.	Flatten out roll and decrease bend in elbow.	One arm, concentrating on the roll and elbow position.	Run through the roll and arm positions on dry land.
The big 'S' - the desired 's' line of the pull is too big (loss of power).	Incorrect line of pull.	Control the pull position.	One arm with flippers and correct arm pull action.	Run through the pull action on dry land.
Feathering hand and arm zig-zag (slips the water).	Lack of strength in the arm or excessive rolling of the body and head.	Keep correct arm position. Control roll and head.	Arms only to build strength.	Build up arm strength by exercise.

Fault	Cause	Correction	Drill	Land Practice
Feathering hand and arm zig-zag (slips the water).	The palm of the hand is cupped or the fingers are open too wide.	Flatten palm / close fingers (a little gap between the fingers is okay).	One arm only, concentrating on the hand and finger position.	Practice sculling the water and feeling the position with the most resistance.
Pull too deep -arm too straight (missing power position).	Excessive roll and arm is too straight.	Flatten out roll and increase bend in elbow.	One arm, concentrating on the roll and elbow position.	Run through the position and action on dry land.
Hands are coming out of the water on the pull through (loss of power).	Incorrect hand positioning, not enough roll and/or the elbow is too bent.	Increase roll, decrease bend in the elbow and move hand away from the body.	One arm, concentrating on the roll, elbow and hand position.	Run through the position and action on dry land.
Hand clapping onto the thigh at the end of the push (missed thrust & causes a pause & delay in recovery).	Failure to complete the push down at the end of the stroke, shoulders not rolling enough.	Change position of push hand, increase roll of shoulder.	One arm, concentrating on raising shoulder as palm pushes down.	Run through the push down and shoulder lift on dry land.

14. Arm exit and recovery

The push through should end in line with, but not against the upper thigh. This maximises the push at the end of the stroke and, by keeping the hand away from the thigh, it allows easy exit of the arm. To prepare for the exit, rotate your hand at the end of the push so that the palm points away from the leg and the thumb points downwards. Your little finger leads the exit from the water to reduce resistance and leads the hand over for the entry. You move the recovering arm in a semicircle straight over the shoulder to the front. Once the arm is back in the water, the cycle repeats with the preparation for the catch.

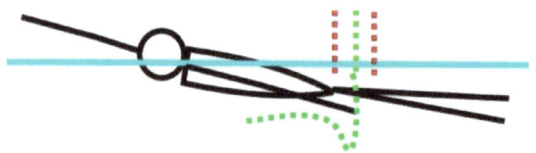

Issue	Likely cause	Remedy	Drills	Out of the water
Exit too short (missing out on the vital power push at the end).	Rushing the stroke and or a lack of power in the arms.	Mark the point of exit on the upper thigh and brush your thumb on your leg to check.	One arm, concentrate on exiting at the desired position.	Exercises to increase arm power.
Excess water is pulled up with the exit (causing drag).	The hand is being brought out of the water incorrectly.	Change hand position ensuring the little finger is leading.	One arm, concentrate on exiting with the little finger first.	Run through the sequence and position on dry land.

Pause on exit - hand seems to hang around in the water before exit (upsets the rhythm and slows forward momentum).	The catch has started too early on the other arm leaving the exiting arm stranded.	Pause hand on entry and check key timing point. Speed up exit.	Slow the stroke down, use flippers to provide power and concentrate on timing point.	Watch other swimmers and check their timing point.
	Failure to complete the push down at the end of the stroke, shoulders not rolling enough.	Make sure there is no clamping of the hand against the thigh, increase roll of shoulder.	One arm and concentrate on push down and lifting the shoulder.	Run through the sequence and position on dry land.
	There may be too many leg kicks within the cycle.	Change the leg kick rate to two less kicks per arm cycle; it will be difficult at first.	Use flippers to provide balance, count the kick rate and reduce until pause rectified.	Watch and count other swimmers' leg kick cycles.
Recovery arm is bent (will lead to incorrect entry position).	Incorrect arm position and not locking the elbow.	Straighten and lock the elbow.	One arm, concentrate on straight arm position and locking the elbow.	Run through position on dry land.
Recovery arm is too slow (upsets the rhythm, causes pauses elsewhere in the stroke).	There may be too many leg kicks within the cycle.	Change the leg kick cycle to two less kicks per arm cycle.	Use flippers to provide balance, count the kick rate and reduce until pause rectified.	Watch and count other swimmers' leg kick cycles.

| | The pull arm is in wrong position or is feathering leading to a delay. | Correct arm pull position and build up strength through practice. | One arm, concentrate on getting the correct pull position. | Increase arm strength. |

15. <u>Legs</u>

The leg movement in backstroke is similar to the kick in front crawl in that the legs are powered by the thigh to move alternately, with one leg kicking upwards while the other leg kicks downwards. Whilst the arms provide more of the power, the legs do assist in contributing to the forward speed and are essential in providing the stability to the body. The usual kicks rate per arm cycle will be 4 or 6.

Kicking is a whole leg activity and whilst you should be bending the leg at the knee; the thigh provides the power. Your ankles should be flexible with your toes pointing backwards away from your body. Keep the feet in the water as much as possible.

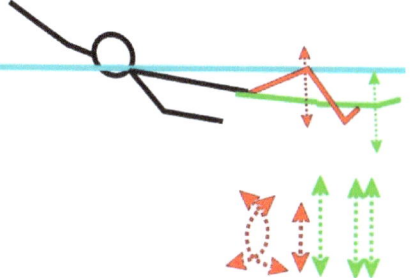

Issue	Likely cause	Remedy	Drills	Out of the water
Crossing feet, usually with one being on the top (inefficient).	Unbalanced stroke caused by excessive roll or deep arm pull on one side.	Correct roll and arm position.	One arm concentrating on correcting pull and roll. Use flippers to make cross over more difficult.	Build up general leg strength.
One leg stays still and acts as a rudder (missing out on power).	Unbalanced stroke caused by excessive roll or deep arm pull on one side.	Correct roll and arm position.	One arm concentrating on correcting pull and roll. Leg kick only to build strength.	Build up general leg strength.

			Use flippers to make cross over more difficult.	
Cycling - excess bending of the knees (leads to a pedalling motion which is ineffective and causes drag).	Kicking from the knee and not using the thigh muscles effectively.	Keep the leg and knee straighter and kick from thigh muscles. Practice a football kicking motion.	Leg kick only to build strength. Leg kick in backstroke position - keep knees in water.	Build up general leg strength. Increase flexibility of ankles.
Weak kick - the kick is under developed (doesn't provide power to the stroke).	Weak leg muscles and incorrect technique.	Increase leg kick rate per stroke. Increase the kick range and drive kick from the thigh muscles.	Leg kick only to build strength. Increase leg kick rate.	Build up general leg strength. Increase flexibility of ankles.
	Too many leg kicks per arm cycle mean the legs can only do a flutter.	Reduce kick rate per cycle.	Full stroke and concentrate on leg kick rates.	Build up general leg strength. Increase flexibility of ankles.
	Too few leg kicks per arm cycle.	Increase kick rate per cycle.	Full stroke and concentrate on leg kick rates.	Build up general leg strength & ankle flexibility.

| Feet at 90 degrees to leg (causes drag and doesn't let the foot work like a flipper). | Lack of flexibility in the ankles. Incorrect position of feet. | Point toes away from body. | Leg kick only to concentrate on foot position. | Increase flexibility of ankles. Build up strength in legs. |

Case study

Nophelia. I started by completing the backstroke card so I could show Nophelia where her stroke was good and where the action did not meet the accepted position.

Nophelia had a wide arm entry with a shallow and straight arm pull round to the thigh. At the end of the pull, Nophelia's hand clapped onto the thigh. On exit, Nophelia was pulling up excess water and the recovery arm was slow. With Nophelia's kick, her knees were coming out of the water and she had a rapid but ineffective flutter kick. Nophelia held her head in a high position and her bottom was lower in the water than it should have been.

I firstly corrected Nophelia's head position by identifying the spot on the head between the crown and the hairline where the water should be and Nophelia did kick only with her arms by her side, moving her head into this position. Nophelia took her swim cap off for this so she could feel the water better. Nophelia concentrated on looking at a point on the ceiling behind where her feet were so she could maintain the correct head position.

I asked Nophelia to come out onto the side of the pool and pretend to kick a football in slow motion whilst she watched the position of her leg and felt her thigh muscles flexing. Back in the pool, Nophelia did a kick only drill with a kickboard held over knees so she could feel her knees hitting the kickboard. We corrected the motion of the kick to use more power from the thighs, as per the football kick exercise, so the knees were no longer hitting the kickboard. Building strength in the thighs will take time, but the technique had been corrected. Nophelia repositioned her body by concentrating on pushing the waist up in the water and this has already been helped by changing the head position.

We then added flippers and repeated the kick drill, arms by the side, so this heightened the feeling on the thigh muscles. We started to use one arm only with the other arm holding the kickboard over the knees as a reminder to keep the kick in the correct position. We concentrated on the correct entry point being the extension of the recovery in a straight line, level with the shoulder. We then introduced the roll to get the desired arm position with a more bent elbow, taking enough time to get each stage embedded.

As the roll has been increased and the arm position changed with an increase in the bend of the elbow, the clamping of the hand to the thigh had almost disappeared. We concentrated on the push down and turning the hand to lead with the little finger on exit which stopped the excess water being pulled up. As the clamping has been stopped, the recovery arm became faster and there was a rhythm developing in the stroke. I checked the leg kicks per cycle and this seemed fine at 4 beats per arm cycle – originally the legs had been making extra kicks at 8 kicks per cycle to compensate for the slow stroke. I reminded Nophelia of the key issues and what to do before each backstroke session.

BREAST STROKE

1. <u>Overall breast stroke theory</u>

Although breaststroke is the slowest of the four official styles in swimming due to the angle of the body against the water, it can be the most difficult to do correctly. It is also often the hardest stroke to teach to swimmers due to the importance of timing and the co-ordination required to move the legs properly.

There are many different styles to swimming breaststroke and it is important for you to be comfortable – see what suits you best and what is the fastest. The arms and legs complete their cycle almost separately with only a small overlap where the arms are being moved forward and the legs start to pull up for their kick. Whereas the front crawl and backstroke rely on a flat body position with a roll to the side, the breaststroke is very much like the fly in that it involves moving through the water in a wave motion to overcome the water resistance.

By contrast to the other strokes, in breaststroke the legs provide more of the power than the arms and this can be up to 70% of the forward motion. The legs are always underwater and the head is underwater for the second half of the stroke. It is good to develop your abdominal muscles to add extra power to the kick.

<u>Key drill set</u> – 'Timing drill'. Working on the basis that timing is so very important to effective breaststroke swimming, the key drill set involves separating the leg cycle from the arm cycle and bringing this together again to meet the key timing point. This drill also isolates the elements of the stroke allowing you to concentrate on each one individually. From the glide position, complete one full arm cycle and return to the glide position, keeping the legs still. Glide for 2 seconds and then complete one leg cycle, keeping the arms extended and still. Do this for a few lengths. For the next two lengths, do the same but only take 1 second glide between the complete arm and leg cycles. You are now starting to move the two elements of the arm cycle and leg cycle together. For the next two lengths complete the arm cycle and then the leg cycle separately but straight after each other. For the next two lengths start the arm cycle and then, as the hands pull round in front of the chest, start the leg cycle by

bringing up your heels to your bottom. Achieving the correct timing will ensure that the backward part of the leg kick happens when the arms are being thrust forward. This helps with the flow of the stroke and maximises the thrust from the legs when the upper body is at its most streamlined. More importantly, the upper body is plunging back into the water which puts the hips in a higher position so the most powerful angle is created for the legs to kick against the water.

Key flexibility bits – shoulders, torso and ankles.

Shoulders. Good flexibility within the shoulders will help the hunch and catch part of the stroke. Mobility exercises such as swinging the arms in a controlled 'windmill' style are good; one arm at a time forward, one arm at a time backwards and then one arm forward and the other backwards at the same time. Once you have completed your work out and you are nicely warmed up (and not before when your flexi bits are cold) stretch the shoulders by placing your arm against a wall and gently rotating your body away.

It is also really useful to have a piece of rope with a series on knots in (for grip) to help flexibility in the shoulders. Hold the rope in a wide position for starters, with both hands in front of you and then move your (straight) arms back over your head holding onto the rope all the way back down to the back of your thighs, and then back to the front. Keep doing this over a period of time and reduce the distance between your hands. In the pool you can increase shoulder flexibility by doing double arm backstroke but please note that excessive double arm backstroke use can cause shoulder soreness for some swimmers.

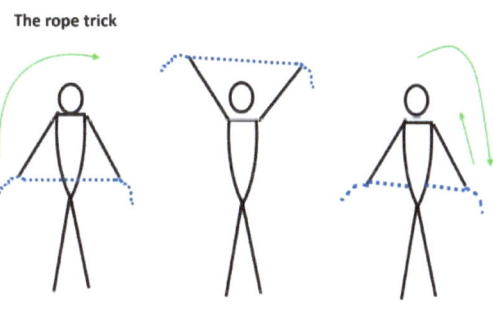
The rope trick

Torso. Good flexibility helps with the back arch and hunch parts of the stroke. Stretching the back by touching your toes (either in a standing position or sat down) is very good. Sitting down doing this is also great for the hamstrings. Remember, stretching should be controlled and you should be warmed up before doing it. You can also increase flexibility in your back by laying on your front and using your arms to lift the upper body, arching your back.

<u>Ankles</u>. Good flexibility within the ankles really allows you to get the best out of your kick as you get more of a range of movement. Simply taking the lower part of your foot in your hand and stretching it down and up will help. Try to stretch into the positions you will need your feet to get into when they do the kick, particularly turning the feet out.

<u>Out of the water.</u> Anything you can do to improve general fitness and strength outside the pool will help you in the pool. The press is littered these days with examples of how swimmers are adding the 1% to their performance by lifting tractor tyres to pulling chains or even taking up ballet. I talk about 'feathering' in this guide as being one of the common technique faults. Feathering is where the arms zig-zag on the pull, slipping the water and this is due to a lack of strength in the muscles which are not able to keep hold of the water and push this past the body. It depends on your age as to what you should be doing in terms of fitness or strength building so I suggest you do your own research and take the advice of your coach.

It is good to understand the stroke position and it is generally easier to do this on dry land. It is particularly useful for swimmers to visualise the stroke and check the positions of the arms for example relative to the body at different parts of the stroke. Try to do this in the correct position where you can – either bending forward or ideally laying horizontally as you would be in the water.

2. <u>Body position and timing</u>

The breaststroke movement starts from the initial position where your body is completely straight with your arms and legs extended. Your back arches as the arms are pulled and then hunches as the arms are pushed forward and the legs begin their backward kick. As the legs kick backwards, the bottom pushes up and the angle caused by the high hip position allows the legs to get into the most powerful position to kick.

Because the body is often at a steep angle it causes more resistance than the other strokes so your body should move in a wave action. The key therefore is to break that resistance and travel through the water effectively by creating a motion similar to a dolphin, 'above' and then 'below' the water.

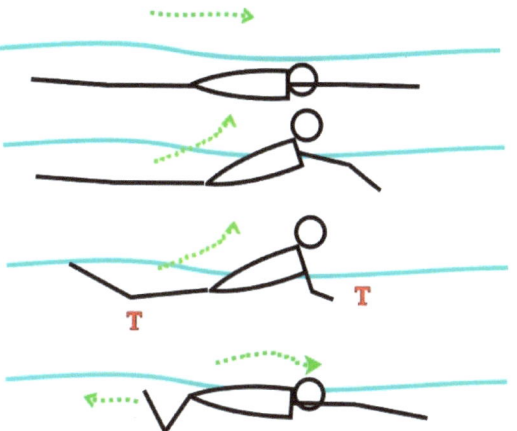

Your pull, outwards and downwards, creates the lift of the upper body which partly rises out of the water. You then 'lean' forward as your arms break the surface of the water on their journey back to the outstretched position. The plunge back into the water is important as it lowers the front of the body which gives the kick a great angle at which to push against the water. After the arms have returned to their forward position and the legs have whipped together, the body is kept in the outstretched position for a short time to utilise the momentum forward you have created. Usually the gliding phase is shorter during 50m and 100m races than when swimming a 200m.

The key timing point is when the arms are scooping around in front of the chest, the heels are brought up in preparation for the backward kick. This means that the backward kick then happens when the arms are being thrust forward. This creates the flow in the stroke and maximises the forward thrust from the legs when the upper body is diving forward and is most streamlined.

Issue	Likely cause	Remedy	Drills	Out of the water
Timing is out (causes overbalancing and slows you down).	Arms being pulled too far back past the line of the shoulders.	Correct arm pull action so the hands stay in front of the chest.	See key drill in 'overall breast stroke theory' section.	Practice arm motion on dry land to get key timing point correct.
The body position is too flat (increases the resistance of the body to the water).	The arms are not creating enough lift by pulling too wide, too shallow and often too far back.	Reposition the arms and practice 'scraping out the bowl' keeping the elbows high.	Sculling arms only or two arm pulls to one kick and concentrate on arm position.	Run through the stroke on dry land. Look at other swimmers' arm pulls.
There is a pause in the stroke - usually after the pull section of the arm cycle (slows momentum and upsets timing).	The arms are being pulled back too far past the chest line.	Keep elbows high and arms in front of chest.	Sculling arms only or two arm pulls to one kick and concentrate on arm position.	Run through the stroke on dry land. Look at other swimmers' arm pulls.
	The legs are starting their cycle too early and are causing drag.	Ensure timing is correct.	Complete 'timing drill' as per intro section.	Run through the stroke on dry land and ensure that timing position is understood.
	The knees are leading when the legs are	Ensure the heels lead when the legs are	Kick only, concentrating on heel movement.	Run through the kick motion on dry land.

| | brought up to the start the backwards kick. | brought up. | | |

3. Head and breathing

You breathe in through your mouth during the in-sweep of the arms when the uplift of your body brings your head out of the water. You breathe out as a steady exhale through the nose during the recovery and gliding phase when your face returns to the water. There is probably no need to hold onto your breath to maximise oxygen consumption between strokes due to the regular breathing pattern. Try to fully exhale as you will change a higher amount of air in your lungs when you breathe next which helps your muscles perform better than you would get with shallow breathing.

Breaststroke can often be swum faster if you are submerged completely, but the rules require your head to break the surface once per cycle (except for the first cycle after the start and each turn). The head should remain static and move up and down as an extension of the spine. As the arms pull up, the head rises slightly and as the arms are thrust forward the head sinks with the chin becoming closer to the chest. The up and down movement of the head should be controlled and the movement itself is not great. As a rough guide, you should be able to fit a tennis ball in the gap between your chin and chest when the head is out of the water.

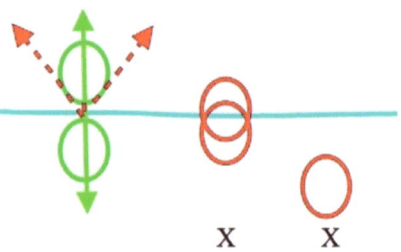

Issue	Likely cause	Remedy	Drills	Out of the water
Excess head movement (upsets rhythm of stroke).	Head compensating for the pull which is going past the chest line.	Correct arm pull so the hands stay in front of the chest.	Two arm pulls to one leg kick, concentrating on arm pull action.	Run through the arm pull on dry land. Hold a tennis ball under the chin to keep the head still.
	Not controlling the head movement.	Concentrate on keeping head still and in line with the spine.	Two kicks to one pull to concentrate on head position.	Hold a tennis ball under chin and run through arm pull.
Head going too far under the water (creates drag and upsets timing of stroke).	Dipping the chin too close/onto the chest and the head is too far down.	Ensure a small gap between chin and chest. Eyes should look forward and not at the bottom of the pool.	Two arm pulls to one leg kick, concentrating on head position.	Place tennis ball under chin and run through arm pull.
	Hand position is incorrect and will be pulling too wide.	Correct hand position and keep elbows high.	Two arm pulls to one leg kick, concentrating on hand position.	Run through the arm pull on dry land.
Ears not going under the water	Lack of plunge and forward glide.	Check arms are providing enough lift.	Two kicks to one pull to concentrate on head	Run through the arm pull on dry land ensuring

(causes the stroke to be too flat which increases water resistance).		Tilt head down slightly on thrust phase of arm recovery and increase glide.	position and plunge.	correct chin position and movement towards chest.
	Lack of an effective leg kick, usually the feet not coming up to the bottom.	Ensure full range of leg kick, heels come up to bottom and knees do not get pulled up.	Legs only or two kicks to one pull, concentrate on full range of leg kick.	Run through kick on dry land concentrating on heel position. Increase leg strength.
Gasping for breath (upsets rhythm of the stroke).	Holding onto the breath until face is back out of the water.	Controlled exhale through the nose and the mouth.	Pull arms only concentrating on exhaling smoothly.	Practice breathing timing within arm cycle.

4. **Arms**

Some coaches will teach the breaststroke arms in three stages being the out-sweep, the in-sweep and the recovery. In that way of teaching, the arm pull starts with the out-sweep (from the streamline position, your palms turn out, the hands separate and the hands move outwards and downwards – the elbows are kept high). The out-sweep turns into the in-sweep (where your hands point down and pull the water backwards until they are in line with your shoulders and your hands come together with facing palms in front of the chest - the elbows are at the side at the body, still in their high position). The recovery follows (the arms are pushed back out to the front, palms together).

In reality though, the out-sweep and in-sweep form one continuous movement which happens so fast it is difficult to split the two. From the start position with your arms stretched out, your palms turn outwards, elbows remain high, hands move to 45 degrees to catch the water and your arms pull back in a semi circular motion as if you are scooping out a bowl. The arms pull back until they reach the line of your shoulders and then sweep inwards in front of the chest. The hands come together, palms in front of and facing the chest and the elbows are at the side at the body, still in their high position.

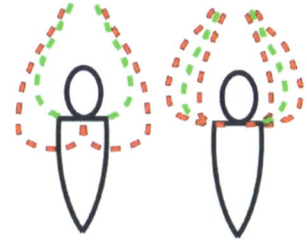

If you use your high elbows as a hinge for the inward sweep of your hands and forearms, you'll create the leverage your abdominal muscles need to bring your hips forward. When your hips move forward, your chest, shoulders and upper back will automatically lift, creating a great body position and wave movement. Pulling past the shoulder line is a common fault and one which causes pauses and unbalances your body.

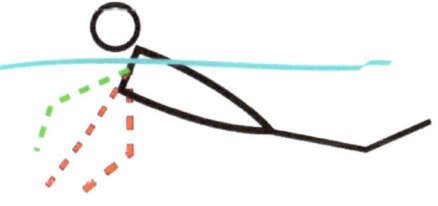

In the recovery phase the hands are 'thrown' forward towards the outstretched position. The elbows are tucked in next to the ribs and then follow your hand line so they don't cause any drag. Some swimmers will recover the arms over the water to reduce drag but this does require more power. Recovering the arms over the water or at least in line with the water level helps keep the upper body high before the plunge which creates the wave action of body. You will need to settle on a recovery style which suits you.

Overall, the arm pull starts slowly to enable you to catch the water, increases speed throughout the pull and the in-sweep and slows down again during recovery. The goal is to produce maximum thrust during the pull and minimum drag during the recovery phase.

Issue	Likely cause	Remedy	Drills	Out of the water
Pull too narrow (missing out on the power part of the stroke).	Wrong arm position.	Wide pull and scooping the bowl.	Arms only or two pulls to one kick concentrating on widening pull.	Run through the stroke position on dry land.
Pull too wide (flattens body, creating drag and causes a pause).	Wrong arm position.	Correct the arm position by narrowing the pull and scooping the bowl.	Arms only or two pulls to one kick concentrating on narrowing arm pull.	Run through the stroke position on dry land.
Pull too far back (unbalances body, stops momentum and causes a pause).	Wrong arm position, pull going back beyond the chest line.	Correct the arm position, keeping hand in front of chest.	Arms only starting with the smallest of sculling actions, then increase the range of the scull.	Run through the stroke position on dry land.

Slipping or feathering the water – hand and arm zig-zag (loss of water and power).	Fingers too wide open allowing water to slip though.	Close fingers (a small gap between the fingers is okay).	Arms only or two pulls to one kick concentrating on keeping fingers closer together.	Swirl water around with fingers open and then closed to see the difference.
	Hands cupped - not presenting the largest surface area to the water.	Open palms and keep the hands flat.	Arms only or two pulls to one kick, concentrate on keeping palms open and hands flat.	Swirl water around with cupped hands and open hands to see the difference.
Limited catch – dropped elbow (loss of water and power).	Incorrect downward and backward movement of the elbows before hand movement starts.	Practice the arm pull and keep the elbows high, move hand and arms before the elbows.	Sculling with arms – small sculls, elbows high. Arms only or two pulls to one kick concentrating on keeping elbows high.	Run through the stroke position on dry land. Check arm position as you pull yourself out of the water – this will be the power position.
Limited catch – hands not catching the water (missing out on pull range).	Hands not moving down to 45 degrees in relation to forearm.	Move hands before rest of arm moves on pull.	Arms only concentrating on correct pull sequence.	Practice sequence on dry land. Build strength in wrists and forearms.

Limited catch – straight arm pull (is difficult, loss of power and can cause shoulder soreness).	Not moving the hands then arms in sequence, not keeping the elbows high.	Concentrate on the stages of movement, keep the elbows high and bent.	Arms only or two arm pulls to one leg kick, concentrating on the stages of the pull.	Check arm position as you pull yourself out of the water – this will be the power position.

5. Legs

The leg movement consists of two phases; bringing the heels into position behind the bottom and the kick, where the legs push out and back before snapping together.

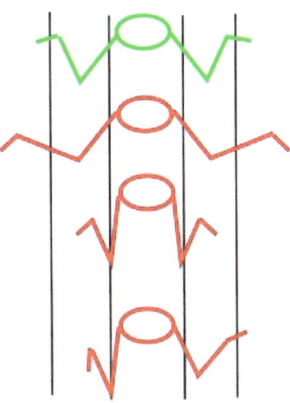

From the initial position with your legs stretched out backward, toes pointed, your heels are moved at the same time towards your bottom with your knees staying close together. You are aiming your heels at your bottom and it is your lower leg which moves the most – not your upper leg which should stay fairly still and straight to avoid causing water resistance. If you complete the movement by using your whole leg, your knees will sink too low and the front of your thighs will be pushing against the water.

Your feet then point outward in preparation for the kick phase and this enables the largest surface are of the legs to be presented to the water. In the kick phase, the legs are kicked outwards and backwards and then snapped together. Your knees will move apart during the kick back as your out-turned feet will be kicking outside the body line for maximum effect.

The legs move slower when bringing the heels into position and move very fast during the kick phase. The goal is to produce the maximum thrust during the kick phase and the minimum drag when the heels are being brought up into position.

Issue	Likely cause	Remedy	Drills	Out of the water
Leg kick too narrow (missing out on the power from the legs kicking outwards as well as backwards).	Wrong kick action with the feet not kicking outside the body lines.	Widen the position of the feet on the kick back.	Legs only concentrating on widening the kick.	Run through the leg kick motion on dry land.
	Timing is out so the kick has to quicken to catch up with arm cycle.	Correct the timing and widen the leg kick.	Complete 'timing drill' (see intro section).	Run through the stroke position on dry land identifying the key timing point.
Leg kick too wide (slows the kick down and upsets timing, causes excess drag).	Wrong kick action with the legs being kicked out too wide.	Narrow the position of the feet on the kick back.	Legs only concentrating on narrowing the kick.	Run through the leg kick motion on dry land.
	Arms pulling too wide and too far back so legs kick wider to compensate.	Correct the arm position.	Arms only, concentrating on the correct position – see pull section.	Run through the stroke position on dry land.
Mini dolphin kick appearing between kicks (illegal manoeuvre)	Arms pulling too far back - creates a pause, unbalances body so	Correct the arm position, keeping the hands in front of the	Arms only starting with small scull actions then increase the range of the	Run through the stroke position on dry land.

		dolphin kick compensates.	chest line and elbows high.	sculls.	
Knees too far down when heels pulled up to bottom (causing drag and lowers leg position).	The whole leg is moving to position heels behind bottom.	Keep upper legs still and concentrate on moving the heels to the bottom and not pulling knees forward.	Legs only concentrating on keeping upper legs still and only moving lower legs. Use pull-boy to lift legs.	Run through the stroke position on dry land.	
Legs not snapping shut at end of kick (missing out on the final power kick).	Wrong action, lack of concentration or a lack of strength in the legs.	Concentrate on squeezing the legs together, build up strength in the legs.	Legs only concentrating on completing the kick and building strength.	Run through the stroke position on dry land. Increase strength of legs.	
	The timing is out, there is not enough of a glide to allow the completion of the leg action.	Correct timing and/or increase glide time.	Complete 'timing drill' (see intro section).	Run through the stroke position on dry land. Increase strength of legs.	
Feet not turning out fully (missing out on the full range and power of	Incorrect action, lack of concentration, lack of flexibility in ankles.	Correct position of feet to ensure they turn out fully. Increase	Legs only concentrating on turning the feet out.	Increase flexibility in ankles.	

the kick).		flexibility.		
'Flipper' kick – feet not turning out, action resembles a fly kick (illegal manoeuvre and does not provide effective kick power).	Incorrect action, lack of concentration, lack of flexibility.	Correct position of feet ensuring the heels are brought up to the bottom fully and then turned out.	Legs only concentrating on pulling the heels up fully and turning the feet out.	Increase flexibility in ankles. Run through turning the feet out fully on dry land.
	Imbalance in shoulders, arms or twisting body causing an uneven kick.	Check and correct any imbalances or twisting.	Two pulls to one kick. Concentrate on keeping arms and shoulders balanced and body in straight line.	Run through the stroke position on dry land. Increase strength of torso. Increase flexibility in ankles.
Screw kick – the leg kick action is not balanced and the action is not in symmetry (illegal manoeuvre)	Incorrect action, lack of concentration	Correct position of legs so they are even. Concentrate on keeping balance at each stage of the kick.	Legs only concentrating on turning the feet out together and keeping the action even.	Run through the kick action on dry land. Increase the strength of the legs and flexibility of the ankles.

| | Twisted body, uneven shoulders or pull or turning head to one side. | Correct any imbalance, twisting or unnecessary movement of the head. | Two pulls to one kick, concentrate on keeping arms and shoulders balanced and body straight. | Run through the stroke position on dry land. Increase strength of torso. |

Case study

Connor. Connor is predominately a fly swimmer with a good individual medley – apart from the breaststroke. The poor breaststroke performance means that Connor is good in the individual medley whereas he could be excellent. I started by assessing Connor's stroke against the assessment cards and marked positions on the check sheets so I could show him where the stroke was good and where it was incorrect.

There was a significant timing issue in Connor's stroke and he almost stopped in the water after the pull and it looked like he was really struggling to recover his arms. Connor had a big head dip, the timing of which did not coincide with thrust forward from the legs. Overall, the stroke appeared disjointed and flat.

The first assessment against the stroke cards showed that Connor had a very narrow arm pull with the arms are being bulled back past the chest line. As Connor started to recover his arms, there was a small dolphin kick and the knees were very low in the water causing drag.

The narrow arms pull means Connor is missing the power position on the pull and is not getting the lift that a wider arm pull would give him. The lack of lift causes Connor's body position to be too flat and there is no wave action to help him get through the water better. The narrow pull is also faster than a correct arm pull so this is upsetting his timing and contributing to the pause in the stroke whilst the legs catch up.

The most important fault to concentrate on is the arms being pulled past the line of the chest which is leading to the pause and the dolphin kick. When Connor's arms are so far back he loses the momentum that his pull has given him when he starts his arm recovery. It's a long way back from where the arms are now positioned and as it is all underwater, it needs a mighty effort and creates a terrific drag. Recovering the arms when the forward momentum has gone, stops you dead in the water. It also takes longer so the timing is affected.

In addition, Connor's upper body sinks slightly as a result of the unbalance of the arms being too far back so the legs do a small dolphin kick to compensate. Connor then starts his leg kick but because his upper body is sinking and he has limited forward momentum, the legs cause even more drag and because he is unbalanced, the knees drop.

I started on dry land and asked Connor to show me his arm pull in the bending position. Connor showed me a near perfect 'scoop the bowl' motion and he had no appreciation just how far back he was pulling his arms. When I repositioned his arms to where he was actually pulling back to, he nearly toppled forward on his own due to the imbalance of the body. I showed him the correct position of the arm pull coming round in front of his shoulders and where his hands should be in relation with his chest. He understood the scooping out the bowl analogy as he had been told this when he was a youngster.

Back in the pool we started on very small sculling actions so he could get the right position for his arm pull. We began sculling using just the hands with the arms outstretched. We then widened this in stages until he found the right position. Connor concentrated on keeping his elbows high as he had a tendency to drop and lead with the elbows.

Then, we started on the timing drill so the arms and legs would start and finish at the right times. From the glide position, Connor completed one full arm cycle and returned to the glide position, keeping the legs still. He then glided for two seconds and then complete one leg cycle, keeping his arms extended and still. He did this for four lengths. For the next two lengths, he did the same but only took a one second glide between the complete arm and leg cycles.

We then started to move the two elements of the arm cycle and leg cycle together towards the key timing point. The next two lengths, Connor completed the arm cycle and then the leg cycle separately but straight after each other. For the next two lengths, Connor started the arm cycle and then as the hands pulled round in front of the chest, he activated the leg kick by bringing up the heels to his bottom. He concentrated on making sure that the backward part of the leg kick happened when the arms were being thrust forward into the glide.

Breaking the stroke down into the elements and then putting it back together was tricky for Connor and we had to start the process over several times as we didn't manage to reach the key timing point on the first few efforts.

Because the imbalance caused by the arms going beyond the chest line had gone, so too had the dolphin kick. Because Connor was lifting his upper body from the whip in on the arm pull, the low knee position had also corrected itself.

The key positions Connor concentrates on in training is keeping his hands in front of his chest and starting his leg kick at the key timing point when his arms whip in to start the recovery. Connor still loses his timing every so often so he goes back to separating the arm pull and leg kick and bringing them closer together again until he reaches the key timing point.

BUTTERFLY

1. <u>Overall butterfly theory</u>

The butterfly is one of the most difficult strokes to do correctly, particularly as it requires strength to overcome the steep position of the body against the water. Technique is ultra important as it is difficult to overcome a lack of technique with brute strength.

There are many different styles to swimming butterfly and it is important to be comfortable – see what suits you best and is the fastest. The arms and legs complete their cycles simultaneously; two kicks to one arm pull cycle. The stroke is continuous and doesn't have the necessary glides front crawl and breaststroke require. The butterfly has a pause only which serves the purpose of giving you enough time to sink your shoulders slightly in preparation for the arms to position themselves for the catch. Shoulders which are slightly lower than the arm position give you valuable leverage when you start the pull.

Whereas the front crawl and backstroke rely on a flat body position with a roll sidewards, the butterfly is very much like the breaststroke in that it involves moving through the water in a wave motion.

In butterfly, the arms provide more of the power with the legs providing a key supporting role in the drive forward (particularly when the arms are recovering) and with creating the wave effect. The legs kick twice per arm cycle; roughly once when the arms enter the water and once when they exit. The legs can be a key factor in getting the timing of the stroke correct and are often overlooked as a driver, particularly when swimmers are learning the fly or perfecting the stroke.

It is good to develop your abdominal muscles to add extra power to the kick and provide support to the arm pull.

<u>Key drill set</u> – choosing the key drill set for butterfly is problematic as most of the drills mean that you are doing something quite different from the actual stroke. The best advice I can give is that you swim normal fly but use short flippers to aid the power and speed of your stroke. Flippers provide the forward momentum to allow you to concentrate on the

individual parts of the stroke that need attention or for you to work on the key timing points.

Butterfly drills using the legs are more straight forward. The variations are using a kickboard with arms outstretched to build leg strength, or arms outstretched in front without the kickboard (aids body movement) or arms by the thighs to build leg strength and concentrate on the timing of the breathing. Short flippers will be useful to build leg strength.

<u>Key flexibility bits</u> – shoulders, torso and ankles.

<u>Shoulders.</u> You'll need good flexibility in the shoulders to swim great butterfly and it will help to keep the double arm recovery, entry and catch smooth. Mobility exercises such as swinging the arms in a controlled 'windmill' style are good- one arm at a time forward, one arm at a time backwards and then one arm forward and the other backwards at the same time. Once you have completed your work out and you are nicely warmed up (and not before when your flexi bits are cold) stretch the shoulders by placing your arm against a wall and gently rotating your body away.

It is also really useful to have a piece of rope with a series on knots in (for grip) to help flexibility in the shoulders. Hold the rope in a wide position for starters, with both hands in front of you and then move your (straight) arms back over your head holding onto the rope all the way back down to the back of your thighs, and then back to the front. Keep doing this over a period of time and reduce the distance between your hands. In the pool you can increase

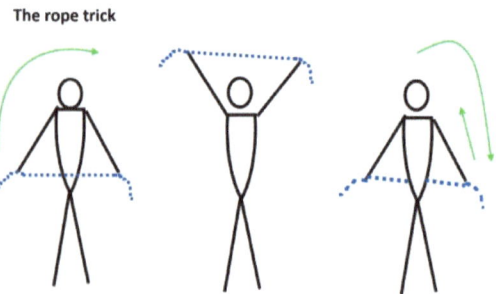

The rope trick

shoulder flexibility by doing double arm backstroke but please note that excessive double arm backstroke can cause shoulder soreness for some swimmers.

<u>Torso.</u> Good flexibility helps with the arching and hunching action in the stroke. Stretching the back by touching your toes (either in a standing position or sat down) is very good. Sitting down doing this is also great for the hamstrings. Remember, stretching should be controlled and you should be warmed up before doing it. You can also increase flexibility in your back by laying on your front and using your arms to lift the upper body, arching your back.

<u>Ankles</u>. Good flexibility within the ankles really allows you to get the best out of your kick as you get more of a range of movement. Simply taking the lower part of your foot in your hand and stretching it down will help. Sitting with your shins on the ground, legs under you with your feet flat under the bottom and moving your body backwards to stretch the ankles is another good flexibility exercise.

<u>Out of the water.</u> Anything you can do to improve general fitness and strength outside the pool will help you in the pool. The press is littered these days with examples of how swimmers are adding the 1% to their performance by lifting tractor tyres to pulling chains or even taking up ballet. I talk about 'feathering' in this guide as being one of the common technique faults. Feathering is where the arms zig-zag on the pull, slipping the water and this is due to a lack of strength in the muscles which are not able to keep hold of the water and push this past the body. It depends on your age as to what you should be doing in terms of fitness or strength building so I suggest you do your own research and take the advice of your coach.

It is good to understand the stroke position and it is generally easier to do this on dry land. It is particularly useful for swimmers to visualise the stroke and check the positions of the arms for example relative to the body at different parts of the stroke. Try to do this in the correct position where you can – either bending forward or ideally laying horizontally as you would be in the water.

2. <u>Body position and timing</u>

The movement starts in the initial position with the body straight, arms and legs extended.

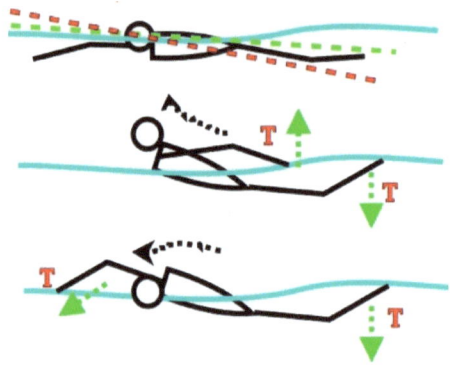

The back arches as the arms are pulled through the water and then hunches as the arms are recovered forward. The body moves in a wave action and is controlled by the core of the body. Because the body is often at a steep angle, it causes more resistance than the other strokes. The key therefore is to break the resistance and travel through the water effectively by creating a motion similar to a dolphin, 'above' and then 'below' the water.

There is no real glide in the butterfly; it is more of a pause to give you enough time to sink your shoulders slightly in preparation for the arms to position themselves for the catch. Shoulders which are slightly lower than the arm position give you valuable leverage when you start the pull. The chest is pressed down by the drop in the shoulders when the arms are outstretched, the hips go up and the bottom breaks the water surface and this transfers into a fluid kick.

Your arms create the upward motion of the body which partly rises out of the water allowing you to breathe without much head movement. The chin drops after the breath and the back hunches to assist the double arm recovery.

The key timing points are when the legs kick down in relation to the arm cycle. The legs generally kick twice per arm cycle, once when the arms are entering the water and once when they exit. The legs can be used as a driver for the timing and if you concentrate on getting the kick right, you can ensure the arm cycle remains continuous. The leg kick you make when the arms are exiting the water is stronger than the leg kick you make as the arms are entering the water. This is because it is easier to effect a stronger kick due to the leverage provided by the more upright position of the body. The stronger leg kick is a good source of forward momentum when the arms are out of the water.

Issue	Likely cause	Remedy	Drills	Out of the water
Timing is out (causes pauses, double head bobbing and breast stroke kicks).	Incorrect arm pull and exit position of hands. Kicks not being made on entry and exit of arms.	Correct faults on pull, exit (see pull and exit sections) and correct timing of kicks.	Use flippers to provide momentum and concentrate on the timing.	Practice arm and leg action on dry land to get key timing point correct.
Legs too low in the water (causes drag and slows you down).	Head position too high. Chin not dropping onto the chest after the breath.	Check and alter the head position if necessary.	Change the head position during training.	Look at the head position of other swimmers.
	The legs aren't kicking enough to provide the forward movement.	Increase the leg kick rate and range to make sure the legs are effective.	Legs only (mix with and without kickboard and flippers) to increase strength and range of kick.	Do leg exercises to build strength and increase ankle flexibility.

The body position is too flat – lack of a wave movement (causes resistance).	The arm pull is not providing enough upward lift of the body or the head is too static.	Correct arm pull and move the chin to the water line and then back onto the chest.	Full stroke with flippers, concentrate on the head position and arm pull.	Practice the head movement and arm position on dry land.
Body is twisting/ uneven arm and shoulder action (illegal manoeuvre).	Lack of power or symmetry in the kick and pull. Excessive head movement.	Correct arm or leg action so it is symmetrical. Ensure the only head movement is up and down.	Use flippers to provide the power and concentrate on keeping the head still and arms and legs symmetrical.	Practice the head movement on dry land and build strength in arms and legs.
Body is too low in the water (causes drag and makes the arm recovery difficult).	Arm pull action is not in the correct position to raise the body.	Correct arm pull action so it produces the body lift.	Use flippers to provide the power and concentrate on the pull.	Practice the head movement on dry land. Build up arm strength.
	Leg kick is not effective.	Ensure two leg kicks to one arm pull and the range is effective.	Leg kick only to increase strength. Use flippers, concentrate on timing of kicks.	Build up leg strength.
Pause in the stroke (upsets the timing of the stroke and causes a loss	The arms are waiting for the leg kick.	Ensure that the leg kick is a continuous motion – they can	Use flippers, concentrate on keeping the leg kick continuous.	Practice the timing of the kicks to the pull cycle.

of momentum).		drive the arms.		
	Needing to take a big breath (as have released the air too quickly).	Hold onto your breath until just before the head rises to take the next breath.	Concentrate on the timing of the exhale during training.	Practice the timing of breathing out on dry land – noting position of arms.
	The arms are getting tangled up at the exit (being pulled too far back, straight up and not to the side).	Check the hand exit sweeps outwards (as a continuous motion into the recovery) and is not straight up.	Use flippers for support and power, concentrate on the sweep outwards on the exit.	Build up arm strength. Practice the arm exit motion.
	The head is not dropping back into the water at the correct time.	Drop the chin onto the chest as arms are around half way through the recovery.	Flippers, concentrate on the timing of the head movement.	Check the timing when the head/ chin drops.

6. Head and breathing

As you start your pull, your hands and forearms will move outwards and backwards from the centre and cause your body to rise towards the surface of the water. As your body rises you can easily lift your chin to fully break the surface and take a breath. Aim to keep your chin on or just above the water line.

You should breathe in through your mouth as you will need to get a great deal of air into your lungs in the short time the movement of your body allows you to. Your head goes back in the water as your arms are around half way through the swing forward. If your head stays out too long, the recovery is hindered and you will cause a pause in the stroke. You should breathe out through your nose when the head is back in the water. If you have great lung capacity, you can breathe out steadily and this helps with the flow of the stroke. I find it is good to keep hold of all that lovely oxygen in my lungs until just before I go to breathe again. Try to breathe deeply as shallow breathing only replaces a smaller amount of oxygen in the lungs.

Normally, a breath is taken every other stroke as this provides you with enough oxygen and helps with the flow of the stroke. Breathing every stroke generally tends to slow you down as the body position is at a steeper angle to the water and it interrupts the rhythm of the stroke. Taking a breath every third stroke can be very demanding. As you progress, you will be able to swim a number of strokes without interrupting the flow by breathing – especially in sprints and out of the start or the turns. It really will be a case of trying various breathing patterns and seeing what works best for you over the distance of your race.

To be able to swim with best results it is important to keep your head controlled when you take a breath. If you lift your head too high, your hips will drop and this will create drag which will slow you down.

The closer your head is to the water the better you swim, but not too close so that you choke on the water. Your head really needs to be controlled during the butterfly and should not move excessively or in jerky movements - particularly to the side. Think of the head as a heavy bowling ball – where your head goes, the body is likely to follow. You wouldn't walk along the street wobbling your head all over the place! Your chin should follow a pattern, going from being on the chest when the arms are recovering to just onto the waterline when your arms are pulling and you are breathing. Your head should be kept in line with your spine and not be turned sideways, especially when breathing as this upsets your stroke balance.

Issue	Likely cause	Remedy	Drills	Out of the water
Head is too high (causes hips to drop, creating drag).	Wrong positioning of the head. Chin not moving between chest and water level.	Reposition the chin on the water line during breathing and on the chest when pulling.	Provide power in the stroke by using flippers and concentrate on chin positions.	Look at chin position of other swimmers, practice chin positioning on dry land.
Excess head movement (causes body to twist, upsets timing and streamlining).	Incorrect head movement. Lack of concentration and practice.	Fix head position to move only up and down in line with the spine, concentrate on the chin position.	Provide power in the stroke by using flippers and concentrate on chin position and head movement.	Try walking along moving the head excessively and see what effect this has on the body.

Long breath (causes a pause in the stroke and affects timing).	There is a pause between the pull and the push slowing stroke down.	Correct arm position and speed up pull, use leg kick to drive the arms.	Use flippers and concentrate on making the arm pull a continuous motion.	Build up general arm strength. Run through pull action on dry land.
	Lack of oxygen, need for more oxygen.	Hold onto breath until just before head raises, breath deeper.	Use flippers and concentrate on breathing deeper and on the timing of exhale.	Practice timing of exhale on dry land.
Breathing to one side (upsets stroke balance and can hinder breathing).	Incorrect positioning of the head.	Fix the head position to move only up and down and concentrate on the chin position.	Provide power in the stroke by using flippers and concentrate on chin position.	Try walking along moving the head excessively and see what effect this has on the body.

7. Arms entry

Your hands should enter the water slightly before the arms with the thumbs and the fore finger first to reduce water resistance. The entry point should be in line with your shoulders. Too wide an entry position means you lose out on the full range of movement in the catch and pull phase as your arms are not in the most powerful position. Too narrow an entry, where the hands touch, isn't a big problem and it is often more comfortable for swimmers with good shoulder flexibility but it can cause a pause in your stroke. If the arm entry motion does not look smooth, then widen the entry position slightly.

Your hands enter the water just before your arms become fully outstretched. Your hands should not be dipping into the water early and 'spooning' up to the outstretched position as this causes excess drag as you are pushing the water with your arms.

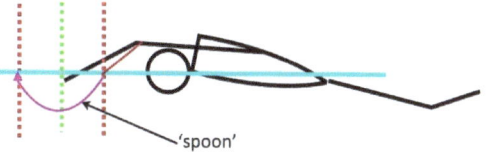

Issue	Likely cause	Remedy	Drills	Out of the water
Entry too short (means missing out on part of catch and pull).	The stroke is being rushed, arms are not extending enough.	Check timing points. Correct entry point by stretching arms.	Use flippers, concentrate on entry position and timing points.	Look at other swimmers. Practice entry on dry land.
Entry too short and arms spoon up (causes drag as hands	Incorrect entry position. The arms are waiting for the second leg	Check timing points. Correct entry by stretching arms. Kick continuously.	Use flippers, concentrate on entry position and timing points.	Look at the timing of other swimmers and their hand entry position.

push the water).	kick to happen.			
Entry too narrow (arms not in the power position and can cause a pause).	You are bringing your arms over too far towards the centre.	Widen arm entry point only if there is a pause or entry motion is not smooth.	Provide power in the stroke by using flippers and concentrate on entry position.	Look at the arm entry position of other swimmers who have a smooth stroke.
Entry too wide (arms not in the most powerful position).	Not bringing your arms over enough to be in line with your shoulders.	Correct entry in line with your shoulders.	Use flippers and concentrate on entry position.	Increase flexibility in the shoulders.
	Leg kick is not providing enough power for full recovery.	Increase the strength of the legs.	Kick only, with or without flippers and kick board.	Build up the leg and torso strength.
	The arm pull is not providing enough lift to aid recovery.	Reposition arms in pull to provide lift.	Use flippers, correct arm pull position.	Build up the arm strength and check arm pull position.
	Head is too high and is interfering with the arm recovery.	Drop the chin onto the chest during the arm recovery.	Use flippers and concentrate on chin positions.	Practice the movement of head to aid arm recovery.

8. Catch

The butterfly pull has three stages, the catch, the pull and the push. Overall, the catch, pull and push follows a keyhole pattern, similar to the 'S' shape in front crawl but a little wider to create the lift of the body for breathing.

From the outstretched arm position, the shoulders sink slightly to give the catch some leverage. Your arm movement starts similarly to the  breast stroke in that the hands and the forearms move slightly outwards and downwards. Your hands will move first; downwards to around 45 degrees and outwards. The forearms move next and the elbows are kept high. It's all about catching as much of the water as possible in this early stage to give you the best advantage. When the hand and forearm are almost 90 degrees to the upper part of the arm, the whole arm starts to move on the pull through.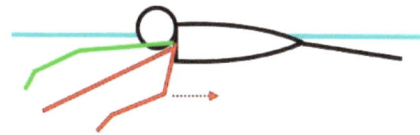

Issue	Likely cause	Remedy	Drills	Out of the water
No catch – straight arm (is difficult, loses the water and can cause shoulder soreness).	Not moving the hands first, then the forearm and maintaining the high position of the elbow.	Concentrate on sequence – hand first, then forearm. Keep the elbow high and still.	Provide power in the stroke by using flippers and concentrate on the sequence of the catch.	Run through the sequence keeping elbow high and still. Build up the forearm muscles.

No catch – dropped elbow (losing the water and losing the power).	Incorrectly, the elbow is the first thing to move and leads the pull.	Concentrate on sequence – hand first, then forearm. Keep the elbow high and still.	Use flippers and concentrate on keeping the elbow high.	Check your elbow position as you climb out of the pool – notice it stays in the same position.
Excess pause before catch (arm stays extended for too long).	The arms are waiting for the second leg kick.	Ensure that the leg kick is a continuous motion to drive the arms.	Use flippers, concentrate on keeping the leg kick continuous.	Practice the timing of the kicks to the pull cycle – slowly at first and then speeding up.
Feathering catch - hand and arm zig-zag (slips the water).	Lack of strength in the arms, fingers too wide apart or palms are cupped.	Close the fingers (a little gap is okay). Keep the palms flat.	Concentrate on keeping to the keyhole S-curve; it will be difficult at first. Practice correct finger and palm positions.	Build up arm strength by exercise.

9. <u>Arm pull</u>

After the catch comes the pull and the push and the arms follow a keyhole shape. In the catch, the hands move wider to provide the lift. In the pull, the hands move inwards to the sides of your body to provide the propulsion forward. During the pull, you should try to get as much of your arm pulling the water as possible as this gives you the power.

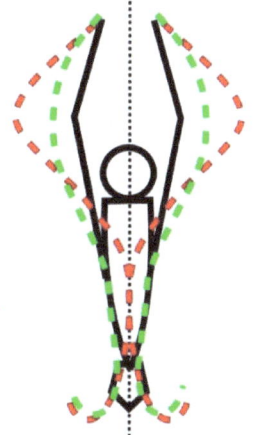

In the push, you push the palms of your hands backward, slightly under your stomach for the narrower part of the keyhole position. At the end of the push, your hands should be moving wider to be in line with the sides of your body to aid exit.

The exit motion of the hands is critical. If you push too far back or straight up, you will stop the momentum and flow of your stroke. You should be looking to push your hands to around the tops of your thigh and the exit motion should be out sideways and not straight up. As your hand position widens at the end of the push – you should carry on that movement to the side and out of the water into the exit and recovery.

The speed of your arms increases throughout pull until the arms are at their fastest at the end of the push. The first part of the pull should be slightly slower as this enables you to get hold of the water. The middle and end part of the pull and the push is where you will have the most power and this part of the stroke should be the fastest. The increased speed at the end of the push is used to help with the recovery.

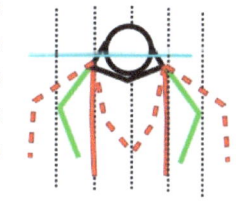

It is important to keep feeling the water on the pull and push to check you are maximising the power. An easy way of checking where your power lies is to look at your arm position when you pull yourself up out of the pool. It's difficult to get yourself out when your arms are too straight, too narrow or too wide.

Issue	Likely cause	Remedy	Drills	Out of the water
Pull too wide (loss of power).	Incorrect hand entry position and pull through.	Correct entry position and follow the keyhole – part of which will be under your stomach.	Use flippers to provide the power and concentrate on positioning of the entry and pull.	Check the position of your arms as you pull yourself out of the water. Increase flexibility in shoulders.
Pull too narrow (loss of power and will cause unbalancing).	Incorrect hand entry position and pull through.	Correct entry position and follow the keyhole – part of which will be wider than your shoulders.	Use flippers to provide the power and concentrate on positioning of the entry and pull.	Look at the arm position of other swimmers. Check the position of your arms as you pull yourself out of the water.
The 'big' keyhole -the desired keyhole line of the pull is too big (you will lose the water and slow stroke down).	Incorrect pull action. Lack of power in the arms. There may be a delay in the leg kick so the arms widen to compensate.	Follow the keyhole shape. Maintain continuous leg kick cycle.	Use flippers, concentrate on correct position. Progressively use the flippers less to build arm strength.	Build arm and shoulder power.

Feathering catch - hand and arm zig-zag (slips the water).	Lack of strength, fingers too wide apart or the palms are cupped.	Close the fingers (a little gap is okay). Keep the palms flat.	Concentrate on keeping to the keyhole S-curve; it will be difficult at first. Practice correct finger and palm positions.	Build up arm strength by exercise.
Pull too deep - arms too straight (loss of power, can be difficult to do and can cause shoulder soreness).	Not keeping the elbow high and still.	Concentrate on the stages of movement – hand first, then forearm. Keep the elbow high and still.	Use flippers, keep the elbow high and still. Follow correct sequence.	Check position of arms as you pull yourself out of the water. Practice the desired position on dry land, marking the angle of your elbow bend.

10. Arm exit and recovery

The exit is critical in keeping the momentum of the stroke going. Not enough of a push then you miss out on a lot of power, pushing too far back or straight up then you will stop the momentum and flow of your stroke. As your hand position widens at the end of the push, you should carry on that movement to the side and out of the water into the exit and recovery.

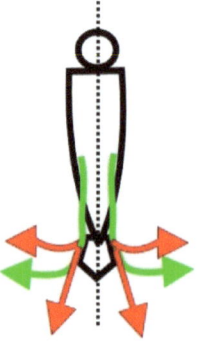

In the recovery, the arms swing sideways just above the water to the front with the elbows slightly bent. The arms should be swung forward from the end of the push in a continuous movement and your second butterfly kick will allow you to do this quickly. If you delay on the recovery then your hips will drop and you will cause a pause in the stroke.

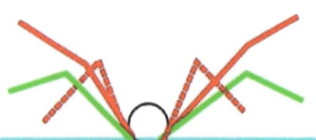

Issue	Likely cause	Remedy	Drills	Out of the water
Exit too short (missing out on the vital power push at the end).	Rushing the stroke and or a lack of power in the arms.	Mark the point of exit on the upper thigh and brush your thumb on your leg to check.	Provide power by using flippers, concentrate on exiting at the desired position.	Mark the desired exit position on the outside of the thighs. Increase arm strength.

Pause on exit - hands hang before exit (causes a pause and often a double head dip).	The push is going too far back or straight up. The hands are not exiting to the side.	Mark point of exit on upper thigh and brush thumb to check. Move hands out to the side on exit.	Provide power by using flippers, concentrate on exiting at the desired position.	Mark the desired exit position on the outside of the thighs. Increase arm strength.
Recovery - arms too high (this is difficult and will interfere with the flow).	Incorrect arm positioning.	Reposition arms closer to the water.	Provide power by using flippers and then concentrate on getting the right arm recovery position.	Watch other swimmers. Practice recovery position on dry land.
Recovery - arms too bent (this is difficult and will interfere with fast recovery needed to keep stroke speed).	Incorrect arm positioning.	Reposition arms keeping elbow bend straighter during recovery.	Provide power by using flippers and then concentrate on getting the right arm recovery position.	Watch other swimmers. Practice recovery position on dry land.
Recovery - arms dragging across water (causes drag).	Lack of lift from pull, lack of power from legs or lack of flexibility in shoulders.	Check and correct pull and kick actions. Increase flexibility in the shoulders.	Use flippers and correct arm action. Kick only to build leg strength. Double arm backstroke.	Increase strength in arms and legs and increase flexibility in shoulders.

11. <u>Legs</u>

The up and down action of your leg movement is similar to that of the front crawl with the thighs providing the power however, your legs need to be kept together and kick at the same time. A smooth undulation of the body fuses the leg kick motion together.

Your legs and feet should be close together to avoid loss of water pressure as you kick. The leg kick is virtually continuous and can drive the overall flow of the stroke and the arms. The power of the kick comes from the lower back, bottom and thigh muscles. Your ankles should be flexible and your toes should be pointed backwards to avoid causing any drag.

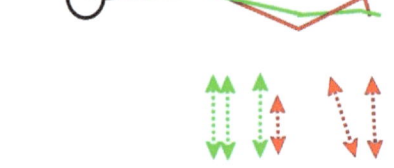

Issue	Likely cause	Remedy	Drills	Out of the water
Breaststroke leg kick - usually when breath has been taken (illegal manoeuvre).	A drop in forward momentum caused by a steep body position as head is too high.	Correct chin positions.	Flippers, concentrate on chin positions.	Increase arm, leg and torso strength.
	When breathing, the push is not being completed.	Ensure push is effective.	Flippers, concentrate on push through.	Increase arm strength.
Knees moving apart (allows water to escape which loses power).	A drop in forward momentum caused by a steep body position as head is too high.	Correct chin positions.	Flippers, concentrate on chin positions.	Increase arm, leg and torso strength.

Legs not staying together and not in unison (loss of power and an illegal manoeuvre).	The body is twisting or the arm action is uneven.	Check that the arm pull and recovery are even and body is not twisting.	Place a band around the knees to keep them together.	Increase arm, leg and torso strength. Increase flexibility in the shoulders.
Excess bending of the knees (ineffective and causes drag).	Incorrectly kicking from the knee and not the thigh or back muscles.	Keep the leg and knee straighter. Practice a football kicking motion.	Leg kick only using flippers to build strength. Kick on back -keep knees in water.	Build up general leg strength. Increase flexibility of ankles.
Weak kick - the kick is under developed (doesn't provide power).	Weak leg muscles and incorrect technique.	Increase leg kick range and increase the kick motion from the thigh muscles.	Leg kick only to build strength and concentrate on increasing the range of the kick.	Build up general leg strength. Increase flexibility of ankles.
Feet at 90 degrees (causes drag).	Lack of flexibility in the ankles. Incorrect position of feet.	Point toes away from body.	Leg kick to concentrate on foot position.	Increase flexibility of ankles.

Case study

Ben. I started by assessing Ben's stroke against the assessment cards and marked positions on the check sheets so I could show him where the stroke was good and where it was incorrect. Ben's arms appeared to be hanging around on the exit and it seemed problematic for him to recover them effectively. The head appeared to do an extra movement up and down before they were recovered to the front. The kick during recovery was a breaststroke kick. The head was twisting to the side and generally appeared to be being held too high. The elbows were dropping and were leading on the catch and the pull.

I started on the head position. Out of the water, I showed Ben the impact of moving his head too much and to the side by asking him to walk up and down moving his head about. Walking in a straight line became a problem and the same sort of thing happens in the pool when the head movement is excessive.

Staying with the head, out of the pool, I showed Ben where his chin position should be – on the chest and then on the water level whilst he was breathing. As a junior swimmer, I had the same issue as Ben with the head and one of my first coaches told me that I needed to be like Frankenstein but remove the bolt in my neck before I did the fly so the chin dropped easily. I got it straight away and still remember this advice some 30 years later when doing a fly set!

Ben told me that he felt he needed to do a big breath to get enough oxygen to keep going. We discussed how Ben was breathing and he started his exhale straight away when his face went back into the water. I suggested that he held onto his breath for a bit and only exhaled just before he was due to take another breath. This would mean that all the lovely oxygen he needed to keep his muscles going remained in his lungs longer. I also suggested that he exhaled fully so that he could fill his lungs with more oxygen.

In the pool, we started to break the stroke down and concentrate on the different elements. Ben put his flippers on to provide support and forward momentum and he completed a set of 25m legs only, arms by his side with lots of rest in between to aid recovery concentrating on the chin movement and exhaling just before his next breath. Once he had got the hang of it, we started to use the arms, again concentrating only on the chin movement and the point of exhale.

I addressed the dropping elbows next. I showed Ben the position the elbows and arms should be in on dry land. I kept his elbow high by placing my finger under his elbow as he started his pull and he concentrated on the sequence of hand first, forearm next. Ben practiced this using flippers and concentrated on the sequence of hand first, then forearm and keeping the elbows high. This was difficult at first and Ben couldn't pick this up straight away so we changed the drill to concentrate on the very first movement in the fly catch. Ben completed very short breaststroke sculls, keeping the elbows high and in the same position and only moving the hands and forearms. Once Ben had got the hang of this, we went back to full stroke (with flippers) and concentrated on keeping to the sequence and the elbows high.

That was it for that session. Next session we recapped the breathing, head movement and keeping the elbows high and the correct sequence. We then moved onto the exit as this was the biggest issue in Ben's stroke. Ben was pulling too far back and coming straight up out of the water. I showed Ben that by pulling too far back; it upset the balance of the body. This was easy to do because as Ben was leaning forward, when he pushed his arms to far back, he toppled forwards. On dry land, Ben marked the correct position of exit on his upper thigh with his thumb and practiced the correct hand movement being from under the body (narrow part of the keyhole) across the top of the thigh sweeping outwards to the side. He then put the flippers on and practiced the exit position and made sure the movement of the arms was continuous. This stopped the additional nod of the head as it no longer needed to compensate for the pause. The final piece was to make sure the leg kick was continuous to drive the timing of the stroke.

Flippers off, Ben did a series of 25m at speed with plenty of rest, concentrating on the hands moving continuously from the push, through the exit and into the recovery. This correct, speedier action, coupled with the improved head position meant that the body position was flatter in the water and the stroke flowed more easily. With the resistance against the water being reduced as his body was no longer at such a steep angle and the continuous arm pull into recovery, the breaststroke leg kick had disappeared.

I reminded Ben before sessions on the points to remember using key words – chin, elbows, sweep out. Out of the water, Ben concentrated on leg and torso strength and the key flexibility exercises on the shoulders, back and ankles.

www.ingramcontent.com/pod-product-compliance
Lightning Source LLC
Chambersburg PA
CBHW042312150426

43200CB00001B/4